# The Best & Brightest
## High School Student's Guide

### How to Choose a College, Prepare for a Career and Find Your Own Definition of Happiness

by ALVIN M. STENZEL

Annie
You've been an "associate,"
a friend, and an inspiration.
Thank you all you did to
make this book possible.
Al Stenzel

Published by PrepWorks Publishing
Dayton, Ohio

Printed in the United States of America

PrepWorks Publishing
P.O. Box 292239
Dayton, Ohio 45429
USA

Publisher's Cataloging in Publication Data
(Prepared by *Catalog Card Company*)

Stenzel, Alvin, M.
The best and brightest high school student's guide: how to choose a college, prepare for a career and find your own definition of happiness / by Alvin M. Stenzel. — Kettering, OH : PrepWorks, 1997.
164 p.

ISBN 0-9660694-3-9

1. High school students. 2. Higher education. 3. College choice. 4. Job hunting. 5. Self-improvement. I. Title. II. Series.
378 — dc12 AACR2

# Acknowledgments

This is a book about high school students, current and prior. They, therefore, are the principal inspiration for what I've written and the people I wish to thank. Michele Hayman was the first to utter the words, "You should write a book!" Her story is mentioned often in this book, and I appreciate the part she played in its creation. Heather Hersh also helped me to realize that I had some important things to say. My Junior Achievement students have been my greatest inspiration. Former Presidents of WE-SEL, the Junior Achievement Company of Wootton High School (Rockville, Maryland) include Sarah Bellenger, Julie Sontag, Annie Bellenger, and Ramsey Janini. Though she never served as President, Lily Chang was "Miss JA" in all other respects. Her reading and reviews of this book's initial manuscript were instrumental in its publication. Kristy Fischer and Elise Rathgeber also helped to point out some important aspects of this book. I thank all the current and prior members of WE-SEL for demonstrating so clearly the talents and enthusiasm of America's best and brightest. Most important of all, I'm proud to thank Kimberly Craigie, my stepdaughter. With mother (and wife) Barbara, the three of us experienced and survived the struggle of today's high school student. For her patience with me and her mother, and her indomitable spirit and determination, I applaud Kim and wish her the best at The Juilliard School in New York. What a wonderful reward for all that hard work.

To all the rest of America's best and brightest high school students, I thank you for being a part of my present and my future. Now go out, get an education, find a good job, and help fund my future Social Security payments!

# Table of Contents

*We are not asking our children to do their own best but to be the best. Education is in danger of becoming a religion based on fear; its doctrine is to compete. The majority of our children are being led to believe that they are doomed to failure in a world which has room only for those at the top. In all our efforts to provide "advantages" we have actually produced the busiest, most competitive, highly pressured and over-organized generation of youngsters in our history — and possibly the unhappiest. We seem hell-bent on eliminating much of childhood.*

**Eda J. LeShan, *The Conspiracy Against Childhood***

# Chapter 1

## Introduction

"Life is difficult." If you're a teenager in high school, I bet you say "Amen" to that. Actually, those words happen to represent a major theme in *The Road Less Traveled* by Dr. M. Scott Peck, a man I see as one of our most interesting modern philosophers. "Life is difficult." Does that mean life is bad, or life is unhappy, or life is an impossible challenge, or even that anything about life is negative? In my opinion, no. But yes, I agree with Dr. Peck. Life is truly difficult.

Recounting the obstacles and challenges that you face today is not pleasant. The most abbreviated list would have to include concern about future job opportunities, the physical dangers that exist on nearly every street in America, and, from what I hear, the decreasing quality of the educational environment in our schools, from elementary schools all the way through our most respected colleges and universities. I can see how it's easy for even the most gifted young person to wonder what lies ahead and begin to lose hope about the possibilities for happiness.

No, I can't wish away the problems that exist, and I won't pretend that they don't make any difference. At this point, I can't even bring myself to pretend that every single young person has the opportunity to be a "success" by the standards with which most people measure success in this country. Possible directions for the most disadvantaged individuals in our society is not a subject I can address in this book. But I believe directions do exist, and I hope what I write here will lead to a better understanding of those directions in the future.

What I can address are the frustrations and fears of those who have the least reason to have them, but who find their pessimism growing every day. I'm talking about you, America's "best and brightest." You are the high school students with the intelligence, the health, and the resources to follow the path of higher education. I'm talking about you, the young people who have the "things" you need to succeed, but may still be depressed, discouraged, and looking for hope in the years that lie ahead.

Magic? No, I don't offer any potion, prescription, or predictions that will make all the difficulties go away, but I can talk about what lies ahead for you. I can tell you what most people twenty years older than you are thinking and how that will affect you when you go to them applying for admission to college or asking them for a job. And I can tell you about being happy and what that may really mean. I hope that will be the best part of what I can share with you.

So I begin without rosy promises of future success and material wealth, without an expectation that all your problems can be solved, without even trying to disagree with the contention that "life is difficult." I begin with a resolve that you're better off than you think. And I promise to give you a few optimistic thoughts to consider while you follow your own best path. Stick around for a few chapters, see if it makes sense. I'll do my best to make it worth your time.

## Stress ...
## Is This What High School's All About?

*Start a program for gifted children, and every parent demands that his child be enrolled. There must be such a thing as a child with average ability, but you can't find a parent who will admit that it is his child.*

**Thomas Bailey, Florida State Superintendent of Schools, *Wall Street Journal***

Isn't high school wonderful? School years are often held out by adults as "the best years of your life." Somehow, it sounds like you're supposed to be extremely satisfied with where you are right now, doesn't it? I don't imagine that's the case. From my discussions with students, both high school and college, and from reading articles about the stress experienced by students of all ages, I certainly don't get the impression that you're all that happy.

For what it's worth, you probably will someday look back on these years as really good ones. If so, then you can try to convince your own kids why it was true. It doesn't really matter right now, does it? OK, let's assume that stress is the primary emotion you are experiencing. Point number one, you're not alone. It seems to be universal. For this small reason, you should feel very normal. Every other student you sit beside every day is either feeling the same stress you feel, or is doing an absolutely great job of denial.

This isn't a bad place to talk for a moment about the nature of stress. In the overall view of life, stress is not a bad thing. Since the earliest cave man had the choice either to throw a spear at an extremely dangerous meal or go hungry that night, stress has been a daily experience for us all. In spite of perpetual efforts to reduce life's stresses, it seems we create as many new stresses each year as we eliminate. It makes you wonder if we're fighting a losing battle.

*[There] is a need to find and sing our own song, to stretch our limbs and shake them in a dance so wild that nothing can roost there, that stirs the yearning for solitary voyage.*

**Barbara Lazear Ascher,**
***Playing After Dark***

While I don't want to minimize the worst stresses that people have to face (daily physical dangers from senseless violence, terminal illnesses, seemingly unchangeable poverty), the majority of life's stresses, even the major ones, are probably meant to exist and have great potential value. One of my strongest beliefs, the one that drives most of the optimism I'm building into this book, is the belief that everything that happens to each of us is an opportunity for learning and for growth. My next higher belief is that our primary goal in life should be to learn and grow. I guess that has a very significant influence on my patience with stress.

Whether the stress relates to passing the English final, getting a date for next Saturday, making the team, or getting into a good college, such ordeals do have the potential to make you stronger for having survived. I realize this theory helps very little while you are feeling major stress, but at least you see where I'm coming from and why I want to help you find ways to deal with the stress.

Most of this book is about reducing stress. It's an effort to help you to know as much as you can about what lies ahead. A reduction in uncertainty is usually the surest step toward a reduction in stress. Once the future is a bit more predictable, stress can be reduced by developing and implementing plans to address the circumstances expected. If nothing else, working diligently toward a reasonable goal can take your mind off the stress. The larger cause of the perceived stress is usually mental, so putting your concentration elsewhere is often one of the best solutions.

In this book, I will attempt to help you gain a perspective for where you are right now. Even in the midst of the stress of high school, there are reasons to feel more comfortable with your position than you probably feel at the moment. I promise not to minimize the effects of the stress you do feel, but I will try to talk you out of some of it. Truth, clear thinking, and basic, hopeful optimism are excellent tools against unnecessary stress. Like any other habit, though, they take practice. Let's work on them.

## Who Am I to Tell You What to Do?

What a wonderful question. Thank you for asking. Actually, my intention is not to tell you anything you have to do. All of this started with a young lady who was referred to me one day by my organization's Human Resources Department to ask whether she should consider becoming an actuary. (An actuary is an insurance mathematician, and that discipline had been one of my earlier career involvements). Michele was interning for the summer at my office and had two more years to go at the University of Virginia before graduating. In spite of doing well in her current line of studies, she was unsure what she should really be studying. Her primary concern was finding exactly the right job when she graduated so she could be happy.

*The reason I always try to meet and know the parents better is because it helps me to forgive their children.*

**Louis Johannot, Master, Institute LeRosey, Switzerland,** ***Life Magazine***

Michele was obviously intelligent, outgoing, attractive, mature, and well supported emotionally by her family. She had everything going for her that anyone could desire. But, in spite of all that, she was unsure of herself. She couldn't see far enough ahead into the future to know whether she was truly on the right road. The pressures and the challenges that lay ahead were, in her opinion, so immense that she felt extreme pressure to make the "right decision" now. Otherwise, it seemed that happiness in the future would be unobtainable and life would be a failure.

Sound familiar? Have you decided that the decisions you make today or tomorrow will insure or prevent your eventual happiness? If not, you're quite unusual, or else you haven't been paying much attention to everyone around you. So I found in talking to my new friend that she was so concerned about making the "right decision" about the future, she wasn't able to be happy in the present, or even to take advantage of the opportunities she had available.

Over several meetings, Michele and I talked about her goals and about the types of jobs available for new college graduates. I explained how I went about reviewing resumes when I had to fill a job opening and the kinds of talents and experiences I usually looked for in an applicant. I told her about my own experiences in a financially-oriented business environment over twenty-five years and about the obstacles and frustrations I faced. I also spoke about the things I had done to create my own opportunities.

We talked about what being happy after college really meant to her. I wanted her to examine her expectations. What was it going to take to make her "happy?" Were those expectations realistic, and even if they were, was she sure that meeting them was going to be sufficient? Our conversations were light, fun, and free-flowing. It was clear I wasn't telling her to "listen to the expert."

*You are never given a wish without also being given the power to make it true. You may have to work for it, however.*

**Richard Bach, Illusions: *Adventures of a Reluctant Messiah***

That brings me back to my original question. Who am I to offer advice? For once, what you're reading is not presented as the opinion of an "expert." I'm not a psychologist. I'm not a guidance counselor. I don't teach students as a profession.

I like to think that I'm removed from the burden of having to be "right." Most experts writing books are expected to have all the answers. I'm not one of those experts, so I don't have to be perfect. I'm free to express my opinions, to let you know what my experiences have been, and to suggest many different approaches to studies and to life. One or more of these suggestions might turn out to be a part of that perfect path for you.

My only claim to fame is that I really have found happiness and success. It was a long, slow path to where I am now, but it was, I believe, a steady upward path that couldn't have turned out any better than it has. To summarize, I'm in my mid forties. I graduated from the University of Richmond in 1973 with a degree in mathematics but am now a Certified Public Accountant. I'm an officer in an organization that manages more than $6 billion in pension and health benefit funds for a nationwide industry. I guess I would say I'm in lower senior management (upper middle management?), and I couldn't be happier with my position. It has some upward potential, but I'm compensated well enough to be comfortable where I am. I supervise twenty people, yet I still spend most of my time brainstorming new ideas and thinking of better ways to do things. I'm challenged by what I do, and I actually like to get out of bed in the morning to go to work.

Not only is work enjoyable, but my home life is grand. I have a wonderful family, including a fantastic stepdaughter Kimberly who recently completed high school. After experiencing all the same stress as you do, she's now a student in dance at The Juilliard School in New York City. All that I write is as much for her as for anyone else. Mentioning my stepdaughter points out that I am married for the second time. I also see that as a positive, because from an experience that didn't turn out as I had expected came immeasurable learning and personal growth. The further you read, the more you'll find that I believe every experience we have is full of incredible opportunities. That may be the greatest lesson you'll find in this book.

*If, when we provide "enrichment" programs, our aim is merely to put pressure on children for accelerated mental development, we may be adding to their feelings of unworthiness rather than relieving those they already have. Instead of focusing our attention on developing readiness for academic achievement promulgating middle-class standards and behavior, we ought to be spending our time and our money on ways in which to help every child feel that he is a person, that he is lovable and that he can contribute something of value to others.*

**Eda J. LeShan, *The Conspiracy Against Childhood***

In addition to my work and my family, I have a wide range of interests that leave me with virtually no time for boredom. At the moment, I am working with high school students in a Junior Achievement program. My personal interests include music, reading, writing, computers, sports, and almost anything that Kim decides interests her (number one is dance). There are few opportunities I wouldn't find interesting, but I obviously can't find the time to be involved in them all.

That list, then, presents my credentials for having something to say that might be of interest to you. Everyone is fascinated by a successful person. How did they do it? Was it mostly luck? Was it the result of hard work? Did it come easily? Was it incredibly difficult? Was every decision the right one? Or could it all have happened very differently? The answer to every one of these questions is "Yes." I will tell you many things, but the first very important point is that there are no "right and perfect" decisions that have to be made in the right way at the right time. Listen to me not to find "the way," but to find that a very simple person can know some very simple, but incredibly important things. My guess is that you already know a lot of those simple but incredibly important things yourself.

When you find yourself saying, "Well, that's pretty obvious. I knew that already," yet you realize a few minutes later that you hadn't thought about that powerful idea in a while, that will be one measure of my success. My own measure of success with my college friend Michele was each time I saw that light of realization go on in her eyes. My favorite comment was, "Wow, that's the same thing my father's been telling me, but it sounds so logical coming from you!" Yes, it happened quite a few times, and thank goodness she didn't write me off immediately. I guess sometimes fathers do make sense, although you're probably better off pretending I am an expert. It'll make it a lot easier to believe what I say.

Anyway, don't expect more from me than one person's ramblings about college, studying, jobs and success. Oh ... and of course, if I can slip it in, a bit about life and being happy. You know, maybe I am more of an expert than I realize. Why don't you be the judge?

## Getting Started

What would you like to know? Based on your position as one of America's "Best and Brightest," I bet your first questions include, "What should I expect in my future? Will I be able to find a good job? What are my chances of being successful?" Excellent questions, but my real hope is that you'll carry those inquiries one step further. How about, "What can I do now to increase my chances of finding a good job and becoming successful?" That's the question I really want to address.

Among the many challenges you'll have in your future is the pursuit of a satisfying and financially rewarding career. It won't be the only important part of building a successful life, and it may not even be the MOST important part, but it will be a significant part of the years that lie ahead. Someday, you'll have to begin by convincing an employer you are the right person for a job you really want.

One of the roles I play in writing this book for you is that of "the employer you'll someday meet when you're applying for your first job after school." I have hired many college graduates into their first "real" jobs, so a large part of this book will tell you what I look for in new graduates. In fact, the next five chapters will cover some of the important evidence you can provide an employer when you apply for that important first job. What I'll include is:

Chapter 2 — You don't need to be a computer expert to get a good job, but knowing what computers are capable of doing will increase your value to any employer.

Chapter 3 — What basic skills do you need just to "get in the door?" How about reading, writing, arithmetic ... and geography?

Chapter 4 — A critical question: Are basic skills enough?

Chapter 5 — Beyond the basics: What are you doing with your life outside of the classroom?

Chapter 6 — Even if you get the job, will you have what it takes to keep it?

By the time you finish with those chapters, you'll have a pretty good idea what preparing for a job really means. Then you'll be ready for the next couple chapters about the major issue I know you can't wait to consider: College. Choosing a college can be quite complicated, but you'll find it gets easier when you see more clearly what you're really trying to accomplish.

Chapter 7 — College as preparation for careers of the future

Chapter 8 — Choosing a college — a mutual selection process

After those chapters, I've got a treat for you. It's kind of a virtual reality trip into "life after college." No, you don't need those funny goggles, and you do have to use a little of your own imagination, but I will help you take a look into those exciting future years. I won't give away the plot quite yet, but I warn you, the word "exciting" may take on some new meaning by the time you're through.

Chapter 9 — The "after school" experience

Chapter 10 — Surviving the "after school" experience

Chapter 11 — Going beyond survival — Having the best of it all

Chapter 12 — Being who you want to be

Chapter 13 — Groundhog Day (I'll explain later)

*You are unique, and if that is not fulfilled, then something has been lost.*

**Martha Graham,** ***Newsweek***

Why do I spend this much time talking about your life after school? It's another part of my effort to help you realize that many things you do now can have an important and positive effect on your future. With a better picture of who you'll want to be ten years from now, you'll find it a lot easier to design the person you want to be right now.

I'll say it now, and again later in a number of ways, no part of your life is separate from the other parts. Some of the best aspects of your success and happiness ten years from now start with the success and happiness you build for yourself today. This book will help you chart a logical, flexible course along that path.

*Teenagers go to college to be with their boyfriends and girlfriends; they go because they can't think of anything else to do; they go because their parents want them to and sometimes because their parents don't want them to; they go to find themselves, or to find a husband, or to get away from home, and sometimes even to find out about the world in which they live.*

**Harold Howe II, former Commissioner of Education,** ***Newsweek***

So ... imagine you're twenty-two years old, and you've just completed an exciting and rewarding four years of college. You had a great time, partied as much as possible, and even managed to go to class pretty often. Now you have the magic degree, and you're ready for the big-time. Are you, really?

I have an open position in my organization that you'd just love to have. Your degree is relevant to the job, and you're convinced you'd be perfect. How are you going to convince me you're my best choice? Oh, by the way, I've got 99 other resumes on my desk from new college graduates wanting "your" job.

Is it obvious yet that a plain vanilla degree, no matter how hard you worked to get it and how much you learned, doesn't set you apart from those other 99 applicants? Can you imagine the challenge I have to find you buried amid all the other "cookie cutter" graduates? Is that the story of your future ... a one in 100 chance of getting the job of your dreams? It doesn't have to be!

Your job, in order to qualify for my job, is to show me how you're a little "different" from all the rest. Look at the word in quotations. Notice what I didn't say. I didn't say better, I said different. Yes, I and every other manager want to hire the best person for the job, and sometimes, we do choose among applicants based solely on their qualifications relevant to the job itself. However, managers learn very quickly that among applicants for almost any position, many will have the minimum qualifications necessary to do the work. In the final selection, what's needed is something that makes you "special" in the manager's eyes. You may be surprised what some of those specialties can be.

*Few have heard of Fra Luca Parioli, the inventor of double-entry bookkeeping; but he has probably had much more influence on human life than has Dante or Michelangelo.*

**Herbert J. Muller, *The Uses of the Past***

# Chapter 2

*Technology is so much fun but we can drown in our technology. The fog of information can drive out knowledge.*

**Daniel J. Boorstin, Librarian of Congress, on computerization of libraries, *NY Times***

## Computing Tomorrow's Opportunities

Want to know the quickest way to get the attention of most managers? The answer is computers.

Twenty-five years ago, I entered the business world as an actuarial student (insurance mathematician, remember?) at a medium-sized insurance company. Insurance companies are very "information intensive" businesses. Insurance companies presented the original need for an automated data base because of their hundreds of thousands of policyholders. When I walked into the industry, no one there had ever heard of a personal computer. In the basement, we had a mainframe computer that took up hundreds of square feet, and we had a computer department with 30-40 people to keep it running. Only the computer specialists understood the first thing about the black box in the basement. None of us "common" workers were expected to understand any more than how to run an adding machine, and believe me, we did a lot of adding.

Insurance clerks were the original "green eyeshade" folks. We prepared 20, 30, even 40 column worksheets by hand, adding columns and rows over and over until everything balanced correctly. Letters, reports, and memos were typed on manual typewriters using carbon paper for extra copies. If there were changes to be made, it meant starting over and retyping the entire document. Sounds like the dark ages, doesn't it?

Now I'm basically still in the same industry, pension and health benefit fund management, but my, how things have changed. We all have PCs on our desks which are electronically linked to each other so we can share files. I even have a computer at home that can talk to my computer at work. I can sit in my den and complete work just as if I were in the office. In fact, the newer PCs are so powerful, my organization, which works with data on hundreds of thousands of beneficiaries, is making plans to do away with our mainframe computer.

The point is not really "how far we've come in so short a time." I realize you want to look ahead to what you need to know. My point is that the computer is the pencil of the future. If you don't know how to use it, you might as well give up hopes of the traditional measures of success, at least in the business world.

OK, you've heard it all before. You've used computers in school, and you know what a word processor is because you had to write papers using one. What I'm saying to you, though, is that what you know about computers at this point is probably like knowing how to pick up a pencil and draw a line on a page. When the time comes, are you going to be able to use that pencil to write War and Peace or are you going to be able to draw a replica of the Mona Lisa?

What I want you to realize is that the future of most jobs and businesses is tied to how they can be completed or managed using a computer. It's not going to be enough to know how to enter data on a computer or print a letter on a PC. You're going to need an understanding of how a computer works. You're going to need to understand what its capabilities may be.

*One geometry cannot be more true than another; it can only be more convenient. Geometry is not true, it is advantageous.*

**Robert M. Pirsig, *Zen and the Art of Motorcycle Maintenance***

So now you're probably getting even more uneasy about what you know and what you need to know. Time out — that's not how I want you to feel. I am going to be using a lot of "shoulds" and "oughtas" as we go through this material. There doesn't seem to be a different way to state a lot of the things I believe. All I can tell you now is,

(1) There are going to be a lot of ways to accomplish what you need to accomplish, and

(2) It doesn't all have to happen before tomorrow morning.

I'm very serious here. Do not let anything I say intimidate or worry you. The purpose of this book is just the opposite. I'm going to suggest a lot of things you may want to consider, but I'm truly attempting to relieve stress, not create it. Read all this with a light heart, and think of it as one person's opinion.

Back to computers. When I started twenty-five years ago, I had never heard of a PC. Now, I'm regarded in my organization as one of the sharpshooters. Why is that positive in relation to you, and what does that mean you should expect from yourself?

Point 1: I went from zero knowledge to being the "idea person" when a new job needs to be done.

Point 2: I didn't do it overnight, it took a gradual accumulation of knowledge over twenty-five years.

Point 3: I can't sit down today and build a computer, or write a system program to make the computer operate differently, or even do much in the way of changing my system configuration so my PC runs more efficiently. Yet, I'm still respected and compensated for being ahead of many.

Unless your field is actually going to be computers (which is not a bad idea, to say the least), you shouldn't ever need to know much about the things I mentioned in Point 3. What you're going to need to know is what the computer is capable of, and what different software applications can do for you. That's not as hard as you might think.

The other important thing to realize is that you can't expect to be, nor do you need to be, an expert overnight. When you get your first job after school, you're not going to be hired as the computer expert. It will probably be a while before anyone expects you to be solving major computer problems. On the other hand, anything you do know up front will be to your benefit. The less training a supervisor has to do, the better.

Remember, you don't have to know everything. You only need to know more than someone else. If you know more about computers than your friends (and competitors), you'll be seen as a winner, whether or not the absolute quantity of what you know is extensive. You'll find it a lot easier to assess your level of knowledge by talking to your friends. If you know more than they do (unless they're real computer nerds), you're probably in good shape.

But don't create unnecessary stress due to improper comparisons. If you have friends who are good with computers, what a wonderful opportunity! I've found that people who love computers are usually dying to tell somebody about the neat things they know how to do. The double benefit here is that you give them a thrill while they make you a more valuable commodity.

Make sure they don't try to start you above your head. If you need introductory training, tell them. All the effort is wasted if you can't understand what they're telling you. If they're not excited about covering the "boring" stuff, make it worth their time. Hire them to teach you the basics. It might take a small fee, or a batch of cookies, or some help from you on their French homework, but I think they'll do it for nothing. It's an ego thing, trust me.

*Skill without imagination is craftsmanship and gives us many useful objects such as wickerwork picnic baskets. Imagination without skill gives us modern art.*

**Tom Stoppard, *Artist Descending a Staircase***

You may not like this suggestion, but it's a good one. Ask your parents if they use computers at work. If they do, ask them how they use them. If you're lucky, you'll get a case study of how they solved a problem by using their computer resources. In case you need an example, I'll put one of my own at the end as an Appendix. It may not be the most exciting reading, but it was so important where I work, virtually everyone above me in the organization eventually heard about how I solved a major challenge with my trusty little PC. It didn't hurt my reputation one bit, either!

One last example. If you've been using fairly up-to-date software these days, you're probably using Windows. That means you're used to turning on the computer and with little more than one or two "mouse clicks," getting into the middle of your word processor or spreadsheet program. You're taking advantage of wonderful shortcuts, but if you have no idea how much basic file management is being done by the Windows software, you don't really understand what the computer is doing. You really ought to learn a bit about whatever operating system your computer is using. You'll understand your computer a lot better and be able to use its capabilities much more aggressively.

So there you are, round one in the effort to understand what lies ahead. I promise it won't be a difficult battle. Computers aren't anything to be scared of if you're a good student. In fact, before you know it, you'll be using your computer to play golf, learn to fly a plane, or to talk to people around the world. These are all very simple things I've learned to do with a computer, and I've only scratched the surface.

*If A equals success, then the formula is A equals X plus Y plus Z.
X is work. Y is play. Z is keep your mouth shut.*

**Albert Einstein, recalled on his death**

*Fearful as reality is, it is less fearful than evasions of reality. Look steadfastly into the slit, pin-pointed malignant eyes of reality as an old-hand trainer dominates his wild beasts.*

**Caitlin Thomas, *Not Quite Posthumous Letter to my Daughter***

*The teacher's task is not to implant facts, but to place the subject to be learned in front of the learner, through sympathy, emotion, imagination and patience to awaken in the learner the restless drive for answers and insights that enlarge the personal life and give it meaning.*

**Nathan M. Pusey, President, Harvard,** ***NY Times***

# Chapter 3

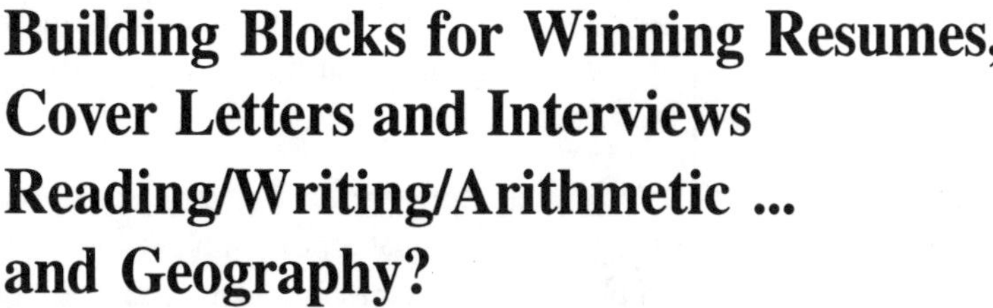

## Building Blocks for Winning Resumes, Cover Letters and Interviews Reading/Writing/Arithmetic ... and Geography?

You'll need to know enough about computers to get an employer interested. What else? I assume that if you're planning to apply for a job in a specific technical industry, your college curriculum will need to include courses relevant to that industry. For instance, if you hope to build a career in accounting, you better take some accounting courses.

But three hundred applicants for your future first job will have taken the same courses. Then what? While few potential employers look at transcripts, and therefore they won't know automatically what else you studied, there are a few things they will try to learn about you. There are also other talents that will impress them, whether they realize it, or not.

Number one is simple. Can you write a decent letter and speak well without tripping over your tongue? I'm not kidding, that's a hidden criteria that people are careful not to emphasize openly. Formal job descriptions don't often list writing and speaking skills, because a lot of jobs can be done without special talent in those areas. It's usually illegal, or at least inappropriate, to require a certain talent if it's not actually necessary in doing the job.

What you need to remember is that we're not talking about a dead-end job without any advancement potential. I'm concerned here with jobs that talented people are competing for, even though they may be basic, entry level, fairly low-paying jobs. If it's a job you're going to be the least bit happy with, you'll probably have some competition for it.

If it's a decent job, you're going to have to apply for it by sending in a written application and resume. Then you'll interview for the job. See what I mean about the writing and speaking requirements? Without being formal job requirements, they become the number one entry criteria before anyone begins to decide whether you can do the job. There are an awful lot of college graduates out there who can "do the job;" what will make you a better choice?

I don't want to imply here that the writing and speaking requirements are unfair criteria. No matter how simple the entry-level job may be, good employers are looking for new employees who will be capable of moving up in the organization. They want talented young people who will most likely be underutilized by the minimal challenges of their first job. Most employers are smart enough to understand what talents a job requires and to realize that there are few entry-level jobs around that can fully challenge a sharp, ambitious young person.

*But it is not hard work which is dreary: it is superficial work. That is always boring in the long run, and it has always seemed strange to me that in our endless discussions about education so little stress is ever laid on the pleasure of becoming an educated person, the enormous interest it adds to life. To be able to be caught up into the world of thought - that is to be educated.*

**Edith Hamilton, quoted in the *Bryn Mawr School Bulletin***

Employers are either looking for minimum competence, hoping the employee will be unable to find anything better and will stay in the job for a long time, or they're looking for the best possible person and will try to find a way to bring them up through the organization. If they're looking for the minimum, they'll screen you out quickly as overqualified, and good riddance to them! If they want the best, then you have to be ready to show them what they want.

The writing criteria comes with the initial application. While most companies have some kind of fill-in-the-blank application, the normal requirement is a resume and a cover letter. The cover letter is not always mentioned, but believe me, it's a requirement if you're competing for a job. First let's talk about the resume.

## The Resume

The main purpose of a resume is to present a basic, easily read, and quickly scannable outline of your background. For a person in midcareer, it's primarily intended to present past work experience. For such a person, it's usually much more important than the cover letter. When you're a new college graduate looking for your first full-time, permanent job, you're not going to have many prior jobs to put on a resume. That will make the cover letter more important for you, at least by comparison. The resume does, however, also include academic background and information about other accomplishments. Even a person without a prior employment history can prepare a resume that communicates valuable information.

When the time comes for you to be concerned about resumes, there are many valuable and relatively inexpensive resume preparation guides on the market. They can tell you more than you'll ever want to know about different approaches to resume preparation. Personally, I don't think the resume is the most significant issue. Except in rare cases, all that's expected of recent graduates is a single page with basic information about "life" to date. Unless you're really into some incredible competition for one of those rare $40,000 - $50,000 entry level positions (no, I don't know where they are, either), a simple single page will do.

In your resume, you'll present information about your academic background and your past work experience, if any. For you, work experience can include any paid employment (even if part-time), or any full-time volunteer positions that you may have held while not in school. Part-time volunteer work is usually shown in a section separate from work experience called Other accomplishments. Other accomplishments include awards, honors, and special activities.

## The Cover Letter

No resume should ever be submitted without a formal cover letter. That cover letter will often be studied more carefully than the resume, so you should spend more time on it than on the basic list of your experience. As a new graduate, you probably won't have a lot of relevant history to put on your resume, so the cover letter will tell as much about you as anything else.

The letter will be your chance to demonstrate many things. The most obvious will be your attention to detail. Is the letter attractive? Is it centered on the page appropriately? Is the type dark enough? I'm not kidding. The first visual impression of the letter presents the first visual impression of you. Are you neat and tastefully dressed? Your letter will paint a picture of you every bit as graphic as a photograph.

Is the letter laid out in separate paragraphs? Does each paragraph have a main concept or does it present related points? Does it have a relevant opening sentence? No, I've never been a high school English teacher (although I do admit I was raised by one.) Your cover letter is one of those places where employers look to see how well you learned exactly what you're studying right now. In fact, they're not usually as concerned about what you say as how you say it. What they (I) look for, and usually won't forgive, are mistakes on the basics such as spelling, grammar, and the most obvious punctuation. The point here is that so many of the things you're learning in high school do have relevance to the challenges you'll face in the future. I know it's sometimes hard to imagine, but I promise you, it's true.

## The Interview

The process of applying for any worthwhile job includes an interview with someone who will evaluate your worthiness for the position. To the greatest extent, that evaluation will involve an assessment of how well you can express yourself. No matter what type of job you want, your ability to communicate with your supervisor will be one of the most critical necessities.

The issue of speech is a sensitive one. Being able to speak well is sometimes interpreted to mean "white, Anglo-Saxon speech patterns with no discernible foreign accent." Although there are still many people who do feel that's the only appropriate speech, this is not what I believe. Your goal in an interview is simply to be able to put your thoughts into smooth-flowing, easy to understand speech.

*The invention of IQ did a great disservice to creativity in education ... Individuality, personality, originality, are too precious to be meddled with by amateur psychiatrists whose patterns for a "wholesome personality" are inevitably their own.*

**Joel H. Hildebrand, Emeritus Professor of Chemistry, University of California, Berkeley, *NY Times***

If your normal, everyday speech patterns do include a great amount of slang or slurred words, or if your speech is heavily accented, you have a challenge. I don't feel it's unfair for employers to expect their employees to be easily understood by supervisors, other employees, and especially, by their customers. Yes, what is clearly acceptable speech in "normal" society may legitimately not be acceptable on the job. You can be assured that the government, through Equal Employment Opportunity Commission regulations, insures that persons are not discriminated against because of racial or ethnic backgrounds. Be aware, though, that regulations which might otherwise address the speech issue will not usually apply where the job itself does involve being able to be understood by others, i.e., jobs involving a great deal of customer contact.

More relevant to this discussion is the fact that in a situation where two individuals are equally qualified for a job in all other ways, the one more easily understood during the job interview will almost always be the person chosen for the job. I'm afraid that's so logical and justifiable that there's little reason to defend any other choice. Accept it as "the way life works," and do what you can now to improve your speech. You're not going to be able to do much to change your natural speech patterns overnight, so work on them now, before you apply for a job.

There is, of course, a lot more to a successful interview than how well you speak. You'll need to show your ability to understand and carry out the responsibilities of the job. For a young person with little work experience, that's often a difficult thing to demonstrate. Realizing that challenge, employers look for other types of life experience that often provide evidence of maturity and ability.

## What Else Can Make a Difference?

*The only place where success comes before work is in a dictionary.*

**Vidal Sassoon, On BBC radio, quoting one of his teachers**

The more you know about many different things, the better off you're going to be. With that in mind, I'm going to list a number of disciplines that in one way or another can be helpful. These are more things that you can't develop overnight, but if you already have an interest or talent in one or more of these areas, you're already a step ahead in developing ways to demonstrate that extra difference in your interview or resume. If you don't have any special interests just now, you're actually at the perfect place and time to begin! We'll talk more about that later, but for now, plan on picking something and having some fun with it.

Over and over I'll remind you: your goal is to be at least a little different from everybody else. Not necessarily better, all you want is a chance to prove that later, but you want to distinguish yourself. When a job decision is being made, you want the decision-maker to think, "Oh yes, she's the one who did that project in ...," or, "I remember him. He's the one who was President of the club in school that ..." It will make a difference.

Having moved beyond my big three recommendations (computers, writing, and speaking), there's not a specific order to my other list of interests. Each one can demonstrate basic intelligence, ambition, dedication to a goal, or a diverse background. These are all things employers are looking for, even if it's not formulated that clearly in their mind. Some of the areas are:

### 1. Mathematics —

No matter how little you think all those required high school math courses relate to your everyday life, you'll be surprised how those areas arise. One simple example I can think of is doing computer spreadsheets. Eventually, you'll run into the need to design a formula for a worksheet that starts to get complicated. Your old algebra equations will actually be of use in solving those types of problems.

Remember the simultaneous equations you hated solving? The theory of "reducing a series of equations or formulas, or even assumptions about any concept, into a logical pattern where all the variables but one are known (or assumed), so that you can solve for the single unknown variable" is possibly the most used thought pattern in decision-making. Understanding how that process really works can make you a much more logical thinker.

*When you stop learning stop listening, stop looking and asking questions, always new questions, then it is time to die . . .*

**Lillian Smith, "Bridges to Other People,"** ***Redbook***

For that matter, remember the theory of logic and the proofs you had to learn? Did you think all you were learning was some mindless pattern of proving a = b? The day will come when you have to recommend a new product or project to your boss. Here's what she's going to want to see.

a. What are you trying to convince me to decide? (Purpose)

b. What information/facts are you giving me? (Givens)

c. What assumptions are you using? (Assumptions)

d. What accepted opinions about the way business works, or about how people act are you using? (Theorems)

e. Show me step by step what your thought process was, so I can be sure you didn't make any bad assumptions or draw any unjustified interim conclusions. (Steps)

f. What is your final recommendation? (Conclusion)

If that's not a frightening reminder of a geometry proof, I don't know what is. What they were actually trying to teach you was how to think logically! I know, I hated those proofs every bit as much as you did, but I now use that thought process almost every day.

Most employers recognize the value of a strong background in mathematics. Whether you use that knowledge directly in your job or simply employ the disciplined, logical thought processes learned by the manipulation of mathematical formulas, your background in mathematics will make you a more valuable employee. I definitely like to see it in the job applicants I interview.

## 2. Geography —

Yes, geography! Come on, it should be obvious that geography is more important now than it's ever been. The information superhighway is almost complete, and the competition is no longer against the company across town, it's against the one on the other side of the globe. If you're sitting in a meeting with your boss and someone asks for opinions on opening a new plant in Helsinki or in Canberra, are you at least going to know what continents they're considering? If they're talking about the merits of the Pacific Rim countries, will you have some idea which ones are being discussed?

If your idea of geography is no more than knowing that the state capital of Maryland is Annapolis, not Baltimore, you're missing a great deal of the information that will drive decisions in the next decade. The basic starting point for understanding the global economy is the globe. That's a starting point you can deal with in a relatively short period of time. Buy a globe or an atlas, and learn where all the countries are. (I know they keep changing, but it's easier to keep up with the changes if you're starting from some basic knowledge.)

Determine what the major cities in each country are. Try to understand at least a little bit of the geological features of the different continents. Which major rivers have influenced where cities grew? Which mountain ranges separated population centers, even within the same countries? In what areas did weather probably play a part in how certain countries developed? You can do a lot of that without any assistance. Just spend a few hours with the globe. You'll be surprised how much more you'll understand about what people are discussing.

## 3. History, Economics, Foreign Languages —

What good topics to follow geography! While each is a discipline that can require years of study to develop expertise, each is important to an understanding of the world around us. It's helpful to know where Moscow is, but that alone is nowhere near enough to enable you to understand why the Russian people are so confused about the transition from Socialism to Democracy.

*Everyone should learn to do one thing supremely well because he likes it, and one thing supremely well because he detests it.*

**B. W. M. Young, Headmaster, Charterhouse School, Godalming, England, *NY Times***

That takes an understanding of hundreds of years of Russian history. It takes an understanding of how incredibly difficult it is to establish a free market system where basic societal assumptions are so different from those we take for granted. And actually to participate in that transition, either to assist in the process, or to take economic advantage of the possibilities that exist, takes the ability to communicate with the Russian people. English alone may not be sufficient.

Can you become a Russian expert overnight? Of course not. That's not the job you're going to apply for any time soon. But would it be valuable to

understand a little about that part of the world, to be able to sit with people who are experts and understand what they're saying? If you were applying for a job with a company trying to sell its products in Russia, what do you think?

I don't care if you're applying for a job sorting product orders or packing the orders in the warehouse for shipping. Any understanding you have about the world in which your company operates can put you ahead of a lot of other people. As I've said, it doesn't take a lot, just a little bit more than your competitor.

## 4. Reading —

Do you read very much? Do you enjoy reading for entertainment? I know, a lot of you will turn up your noses, but putting your nose in a book instead will help you a lot more.

If it helps any, I'm not even talking about dry, intellectual books, although it's even possible to enjoy those once you get into the habit. I would be happy if you did any significant reading on a regular basis. Anything you read has at least some value if it makes you look beyond what you already know. The trashiest romance novels often have an interesting setting. You'll learn more geography from one of those novels than you will from most television situation comedies.

A historical romance, or any historical fiction, will teach you a lot about history, other societies, maybe even economics, foreign languages; you never know until you open the book. Some of the best science fiction can open your mind to technologies already in development. Political, espionage, medical, and high finance thrillers all teach incredible amounts about how societies work. It's very hard not to learn something when you read, no matter how much you're reading "just for fun."

*Nothing I do can't be done by a 10 year old ... with 15 years of practice.*

**Harry Blackstone, Jr., on being a magician,** ***Newsweek***

The only caution I'll give you about reading is to be aware of "sound bite" journalism. It's important to read newspapers and news magazines, and it's fine to read one-sided or opinionated material, as long as you understand what you're being fed. In most cases, those sources are like fast food. They're easy to find, inexpensive, can be eaten quickly, and do provide basic nourishment. But they don't provide a well-rounded diet, they don't lead you to try new things, and they don't promote strong-willed self-reliance.

*A guidance counselor who has made a fetish of security, or who has unwittingly surrendered his thinking to economic determinism, may steer a youth away from his dream of becoming a poet, an artist, a musician, or any other of thousands of things, because it offers no security, it does not pay well, there are no vacancies, it has no 'future.'*

**Henry M. Wriston, President Emeritus, Brown University, *Wall Street Journal***

If you can read the entire news piece or article in ten minutes or less, news is all you're getting. You need a bigger, healthier serving if you're going to grow. If you want an example of what I mean by a healthy serving, something between a typical news magazine and a full length book, pick up a copy of the *Atlantic Monthly*. You'll see what in-depth writing really means. In my opinion, it's the best magazine on the market, with nothing else in second place. I'll talk more about it later, but it's a winner for the serious reader. The *Atlantic Monthly* is a challenge, I admit, but a worthwhile one.

Oh yes, one more thought if the reading idea seems like a lot to handle. Start with going to the movies or renting them. Compared to reading, however, with movies you do have to be a little more selective if you're hoping for some worthwhile enlightenment. I doubt the typical horror/slasher epic is going to help you. (In fact, there are reasons to worry if that's a regular diet for you.)

If you're going to make movies a starting point for expanding your view of the world, go back and look at the last few pages about reading material. Find a movie based on a book that I would have suggested you read. Watch the movie for fun, but take notice of the setting. What environment supports the story? What geography, history, economics, society, language, and basic assumptions drive the characters? As a perfect example, try *The Hunt for Red October*. Even if you've already seen it, watch it again from your new perspective. If your movie watching can become more focused, you'll begin to gain more of value to your overall life and become more valuable to a potential employer.

No, you probably can't list "movie addict" on your resume, but if you can write a movie review and get it published somewhere, your interest in movies can become as impressive a special interest as having won a prize in the science fair. You're demonstrating initiative and the desire to participate in and learn from the world around you. There are no limits to the ways in which initiative can be shown. Just get involved in life, any way you can.

*The essence of our effort to see that every child has a chance must be to assure each an opportunity, not to become equal, but to become different - to realize whatever unique potential of body, mind and spirit he or she possesses.*

**John Fischer, Dean, Teacher's College, Columbia Univ., *San Francisco Examiner***

# Chapter 4

## Are Basic Skills All You Really Need?

High school offers you opportunities to develop an important range of skills and talents. I hope I've already helped you see how the effort you expend now truly will be of value throughout your life. But, are those subjects ... reading, writing, mathematics, and all the other course work you study, enough to prepare you for the future? When you leave school, either after high school or after college, will your studies have given you all the preparation you need to be a success in the adult world?

Preparing students for the workforce is a much bigger concern among adults than you may believe. This chapter will show you how serious many, many people are about helping you become the worker, the employee, the person you want to be. This story begins over seven years ago. In April 1991, President George Bush called for the development of World Class Standards for educational performance as he announced a new educational strategy, "AMERICA 2000." In preparation for that announcement, as the first important step in understanding what "standards for educational strategy" might really mean, the President appointed a commission to investigate what the workforce needed from its workers. From your perspective, the question might more appropriately be, "What do students entering the workforce need to know to be successful?" You may be surprised at the answers the commission found.

## SCANS— What Work Requires of Schools

Lynn Martin, Secretary of Labor was charged with organizing a commission to be called SCANS - "The Secretary's Commission on Achieving Necessary Skills." This group of almost thirty representatives from important businesses, school districts, labor unions, and other organizations spent 12 months talking to business owners, to public employers, to the people who manage employees daily, to union officials, and to workers on the line and at their desks. They talked to people in stores, shops, government offices, and manufacturing facilities. What did they learn?

In the cover letter to the initial Report, Secretary Martin and the Commission noted, "Good jobs depend on people who can put knowledge to work. New workers must be creative and responsible problem solvers and have the skills and attitudes on which employers can build. Traditional jobs are changing and new jobs are created everyday. High paying but unskilled jobs are disappearing. Employers and employees share the belief that all workplaces must 'work smarter.'"

*Most certification today is pure "credentialism." [It] must begin to reflect our demand for excellence, not our appreciation of parchment.*

**William J. Bennett, U.S. Secretary of Education,** ***NY Times***

The Report itself is fascinating. I'd love for you to get a copy and read it all, but I know most of you will not have time for that. What I do want you to understand is that the skills I've talked about in the last couple chapters are not, by themselves, all that you will need as you move ahead toward your future. Before I move on to additional specific suggestions, let's take a quick look at the Executive Summary of the SCANS Report. It will set the stage for some of the next things I have to tell you.

## The SCANS Competencies, Skills and Personal Qualities

The SCANS Commission had a grand vision, but a specific focus. In their opening statement to parents, employers, and educators, they tried to identify these saying, "We understand that schools do more than simply prepare people to make a living. They prepare people to live full lives — to participate in their communities, to raise families, and to enjoy the leisure that is the fruit of their labor. A solid education is its own reward. This report concerns only one part of that education, the part that involves how schools prepare young people for work."

The Commission's work was solely focused on helping all of us understand what businesses want from their employees, in the hope and expectation that schools would endeavor to help students prepare to meet those needs. From its research, the Commission reached three major conclusions:

1. All American high school students must develop a new set of competencies and foundation skills if they are to enjoy a productive, full and satisfying life.

2. The qualities of high performance that today characterize our most competitive companies must become the standard for the vast majority of our companies, large and small, local and global.

3. The nation's schools must be transformed into high-performance organizations in their own right.

The clearest statement of the Commission's conclusions are the five competencies and the three-part foundation of skills and personal qualities that the Commission identified as lying at, "the heart of job performance today. These eight areas," the Commission noted, "represent essential preparation for all students, both those going directly to work and those planning further education. All eight must be an integral part of every young person's school life."

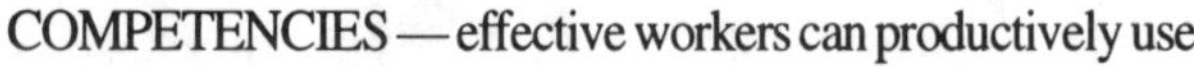

COMPETENCIES — effective workers can productively use:

I. Resources — allocating time, money, materials, space, and staff;

II. Interpersonal Skills — working on teams, teaching others, serving customers, leading, negotiating, and working well with people from culturally diverse backgrounds;

III. Information — acquiring and evaluating data, organizing and maintaining files, interpreting and communicating, and using computers to process information;

IV. Systems — understanding social, organizational, and technological systems; monitoring and correcting performance, and designing or improving systems;

V. Technology — selecting equipment and tools, applying technology to specific tasks, and maintaining and troubleshooting technologies.

*The quality of a university is measured more by the kind of student it turns out than the kind it takes in.*

**Robert J. Kibbee, City University of NY,** ***NY Times***

THE FOUNDATIONS — competence requires:

I. Basic Skills — reading, writing, arithmetic and mathematics, speaking, and listening;

II. Thinking Skills — thinking creatively, making decisions, solving problems, seeing things in the mind's eye, knowing how to learn, and reasoning;

III. Personal Qualities — individual responsibility, self-esteem, sociability, self-management, and integrity.

Pretty intimidating, isn't it? Do you feel prepared to meet all those criteria? I'm not even sure I do! A better question might be, is your school preparing you to meet those criteria? I bet your answer to that question is also, "No!"

## Are Schools Trying to Meet Your Needs?

*The greatest danger of traditional education is that learning may remain purely verbal. Words are learned and placed in dead storage in one part of the mind while life is lived unilluminated and unguided by this learning. Such a danger is inherent in the very nature of education.*

**Mirra Komarovsky, *Women in the Modern World***

What do you think you're supposed to be learning in school? No, I really don't expect you to have a perfect answer. In fact, no adults have that perfect answer, either. Some adults, and some school systems, believe that the recommendations in the SCANS report are right on target. They're already in the middle of redesigning your curriculum to address those competencies and foundations. On the other hand, some adults, and some other school systems, believe you're in school to learn the basics. Reading, writing, and arithmetic are so important, they can't be emphasized less to make room for other teaching goals.

Who's right? Like nearly every other question you'll face in this world, the answer is likely to be, "it depends." The other most frequent answer is, "Each person has to make their own decision." Those two answers account for the fact that few school systems have fully implemented the SCANS Commission's recommendations. If variations in personal beliefs weren't enough reason for your schools not to have changed much because of the SCANS Commission, just try to imagine how you would change your classes to teach the competencies I've listed.

Can you envision learning in your math class how to, "acquire and evaluate data, organize and maintain files, and interpret and communicate information?" How about your history class? Will you learn there how to, "understand social, organizational, and technological systems, monitor and correct performance, and design or improve such systems?" If you're really sharp, you may see some possibilities, but I doubt your current classes are accomplishing those lofty goals. As hard as adults are working to design your classes to teach you what you need to know, and I promise they really are trying, I'm sure you can see how far there still is to go.

## What Can You Do to Help Yourself?

*A man is not finished when he is defeated. He is finished when he quits.*

**Richard M. Nixon,**
***Dallas Times-Herald***

The facts I've presented leave you in a difficult position. My twenty-five years in the corporate world verify for me that the SCANS Commission did a good job. I agree quite strongly with their identification of the competencies and skills I want to see in a new employee. But if you can't learn all those things in school, what other options do you have?

If you look again at the SCANS criteria, there are a few basic concepts that summarize what an employer wants. Understand those and your goals are that much simpler. My analysis of the SCANS criteria is as follows:

a. You need the basics — Foundation I.

b. You need to understand how technology, including computers, can be used to solve problems — Competencies III. and V.

c. You need to know how organizations and individuals work together to accomplish goals — Competencies I., II., and IV.

d. You need to be a person who understands these three sets of skills, who can see the "big picture," and who has the personal qualities that others, including employers, will respect — Foundations II. and III.

The big questions then become, "Do you have the resources to gain all of these skills? If so, how do you find and use these resources?"

I covered "a" (the basics) in Chapter 3. I covered "b" (computers) in Chapter 2. Remember, I didn't say you had to know how to program a computer, or how to make it run more efficiently. You only need to understand its capabilities. You can learn that by reading a few interesting books about technology or even by talking with your parents and their friends.

The bigger challenge involves learning the skills and developing the personal qualities described in "c" and "d." There aren't many high schools that have been able to design those learning experiences into their regular classroom instruction.

The problem, then, is that you may not be able to learn these skills in the classroom. Fortunately, there are unlimited opportunities to learn everything you need ... outside the classroom. The next chapter will show you how easy, and how much fun, it can be.

*The ability to think straight, some knowledge of the past, some vision of the future, some skill to do useful service, some urge to fit that service into the well-being of the community, these are the most vital things education must try to produce.*

**Virginia Gildersleeve, Dean Emeritus, Barnard College,**
***Many a Good Crusade***

# Chapter 5

## What Are You Doing with Your Life Outside of School?

If you accept my contention that what you learn in the classroom is not all that you need to prepare for your future, where else do you turn for help? What else will show an employer (or a college admissions officer) your special talents, your concern with a perspective larger than your own personal welfare? There are ways to accomplish this while finding incredible growth as an individual, with all the rewards in self-image that will last far beyond college admission or a first job. Involvement in volunteer services or participation in special interest activities can make a great difference in your life.

## School-related Activities

*All education is, in a sense, vocational, vocational for living.*

**Sir John Newsom, "The Education Women Need,"** ***Observer***

Maintaining your grades in high school or college can take a tremendous amount of time and energy. A narrow focus on nothing but grades, however, will probably do you more harm than good. If you want to learn more about life, improve your own ability to deal with challenges, and prepare yourself to be what an employer wants, you need something in your life beyond what you can read in a book or hear in a classroom.

Getting involved in an activity outside of the classroom can add immense value to many aspects of your life, both present and future. There are so many opportunities, I hardly know where to begin. My daughter's high school has more than 70 different clubs, activities, and special interest groups, and that doesn't include the athletic programs, which can be just as valuable. Each one offers the chance to learn new talents, to experience personal responsibility, to try one's hand at leadership, or simply to have some fun. Participation in an activity, if taken seriously and worked at diligently, can become a satisfying focal point in a young life.

For me, during my high school years, the activity was the school band. I was a good student, but it was band practice that got me to school every morning. I made most of my friends in band class and during band activities. I still have the warmest memories of marching in parades and at football games, and performing in concerts. Even though I wasn't highly talented, I tried out for and earned the chance to be a member of the regional high school band for three years. My greatest high school treasures are the record albums recorded at my band's concerts.

My high school band wasn't one of the best in the area, but we had a great time. I learned how to play a role in a large group where success depended on teamwork. I learned how to be supportive of others, because their success was important to my own. I had the opportunity to travel around the area where I lived, meeting people from other schools, and making many new friends. It brought an enjoyable focus to my life that studying just couldn't create. I don't think I realized at the time how happy participation in the band program enabled me to be.

*Most of the important experiences that truly educate cannot be arranged ahead of time with any precision.*

**Harold Taylor, President, Sarah Lawrence College, "The Private World of the Man with the Book," *Saturday Review***

Funniest of all, and hopefully instructive to you, my first job interview after college was probably successful because the boss and I found that we had played the same musical instrument in school. Coincidence? Sure it was, but the point is exactly what I want you to understand. My background outside of the classroom had relevance to someone with an influence on my success. He understood the importance of what I had experienced and knew that I would probably be a good employee. He understood something about me that grades and degrees couldn't tell. I had demonstrated qualities through my participation in the band that he admired from firsthand experience. It made me special in his eyes, and he gave me the break I needed.

Will an activity in which you participate earn you a job in the same way? Possibly not, but it will gain for you the type of experiences the band helped me find. Some employer, somewhere, will understand what you've learned through that activity, and it will make a difference.

I don't want to overemphasize the job-related benefits, to the exclusion of the "happiness" benefits. I might even place the latter as more important. As I mentioned, the band was what got me to school in the morning. It even saved my life. One morning my junior year, one of my best friends decided to skip school and asked me to go with him. I thought about it seriously, although I'd never done it before, but declined because I didn't want to miss band practice. Two hours later, his car was hit by a train at a crossing and he was dead. I could have been with him.

The way I look at it, I had something in my life more important than the momentary thrill of skipping school. Today's equivalent would probably be having something more important than getting involved in drugs, or more important than hanging around with the "wrong crowd" after school. Activities are things that are almost always available to every student. There are really few excuses for not finding something to make life more rewarding.

*The opposite of love is not hate, it's indifference.*
*The opposite of art is not ugliness, it's indifference.*
*The opposite of faith is not heresy, it's indifference.*
*And the opposite of life is not death, it's indifference.*

**Elie Wiesel,**
***US News & World Report***

## Volunteer Activities

Want to combine the kind of personal growth that comes from school-related activities with an even higher purpose? Why not consider volunteering with an organization that provides some valuable service to the community. Again, the number of opportunities are almost endless, and the advantages you can gain are just as extensive.

On a material basis, volunteer work shows employers many things they like to see in potential employees. No matter what the area of service may be, the experience says to employers that the job applicant is a person who cares about more than just their own personal gain. An individual who is willing to give more than they expect to receive in their personal life might carry over that selflessness into the business environment. As I've said, that's exactly what an employer needs to find.

The more involved a person has been in volunteer activities, the more likely that he or she has learned how to take on a leadership role. As the truest measure of leadership is the ability to get people to work together, to convince them to sacrifice some of their own personal desires for the good of the larger group, successful leadership in a volunteer activity is a good measure of leadership potential in a work environment. In my opinion, dedicated, successful experience in a volunteer capacity is more impressive than a "for pay" work experience. It says more to me about the person "as a person." Wise employers value the wide background demonstrated by volunteer activities.

The greater benefit to volunteer activities, however, is the personal growth that nearly always occurs. There's something special that happens inside when you expend effort on behalf of another. If that effort has the result of helping another person grow in self respect, the effort actually approaches the definition Dr. M. Scott Peck uses for Love. If your goal is not only to find a good job, but to find a good life, then giving of yourself in a volunteer effort will go a long way toward helping you find both.

My first real volunteer activity didn't occur until I was out of college. I was already working in my first job when a friend asked me to join the local Jaycees chapter. The Jaycees (Junior Chamber of Commerce) was a service organization of young men age 35 or younger. They carried out many different service projects, including assisting the American Heart Association in teaching cardiopulmonary resuscitation (CPR). My friend was a CPR instructor and he encouraged me to take the course. I enjoyed learning the lifesaving techniques so much, he tried to convince me to become an instructor.

I was so scared about the idea of talking in front of a group that it took a lot of convincing, but they needed instructors. By the time my CPR career was finished, I became an instructor, I became an instructor-trainer (I taught people how to teach people), I became a member of the Heart Association's state affiliate faculty for CPR (I taught people how to teach people how to teach people), and I earned a place on the Board of Directors of the Richmond, Virginia chapter of the American Heart Association. A lifetime achievement? No, that was all accomplished in about four or five years.

*Much that passes for education . . . is not education at all, but ritual. The fact is that we are being educated when we know it the least.*

**David P. Gardner, President, Univ. Of Utah, Salt Lake City,** ***Vital Speeches***

Believe it or not, that's usually the nature of volunteer work. If you have the interest and the talent, the opportunities are there. In a relatively short period of time, you can become almost anything you want. There's never enough help.

Want to run an organization instead of starting at the bottom? I helped to establish a local chapter of a national insurance educational organization. I also volunteered to be the Treasurer of the Employee Credit Union where I worked and ended up as its President for several years. Those were opportunities that I took on when almost no one else wanted to do them. They were great fun while I worked on them, I learned a lot, and I probably don't have to tell you how good they looked on my resume whenever I decided to change jobs.

After those experiences, I spent five years on the Board of Directors of a United Way supported organization that recruits, trains, and refers volunteers to other organizations who need their services. It makes it easy to see why I believe in volunteer service, doesn't it?

My final example is my current activity. It somehow wraps all I've said about activities into a nice package. I now serve as leader for a high school Junior Achievement program (see Appendix B). Junior Achievement assists teenagers in creating their own officially chartered company.

*There is a real magic in enthusiasm. It spells the difference between mediocrity and accomplishment. It gives warmth and good feeling to all your personal relationships.*

**Norman Vincent Peale, "Confident Living,"** ***NY Herald Tribune***

They sell stock in their company, open a checking account, choose, assemble, and sell products, and they pay themselves commissions and salaries. At the end of the school year, they liquidate the company and pay the stockholders back their investment with dividends. During the year, in addition to running their own company, they learn about the American economy, the stock market, and many other business related topics.

What do the company members get out of the program? First, they have a great time, and they get to earn some real money. Second, in a setting different from their daytime school classes, they get to learn some important lessons about how businesses operate. In addition, the program offers competition with other Junior Achievement companies, trips and conventions, and special consideration in many scholarship competitions.

Most important, the students get to feel the true challenge of being dependent on each other for success. With only minimal necessary direction from advisors, leaders emerge among the students. They find the need for self discipline and group discipline, a freedom not as wonderful as they might have thought. They find the tangible rewards of hard work, and the frustrating penalties of disorganization.

To an extent, they learn a bit about what it's like to be an adult in the business world. It can be an eye-opening experience, for the advisors as well as the students. If any adults think young people aren't capable of great accomplishments, give them the resources and the training to run their own business and step back. You may be quite surprised at the result.

If you were an employer looking to hire a new college graduate for a business position, how would you feel about a person with Junior Achievement experience? Would you think they might have more appreciation for what goes on in your organization than someone without such experience? I bet you would. That experience was something not available in school.

And last of all, what about the benefits for me, the advisor. Even at my "advanced" age, working with the young people has brought many rewards. I've learned even more than I knew about organization and thoroughness. I've gained a new faith in the future of young people. And in the biggest surprise from my latest volunteer activity, I've found I have something to say to young people that goes far beyond what I realized I had in me. Yes, I've learned more about myself, helped a few people in a small way, and maybe, through this book, found a way to help many more. You never know where a small effort will lead, do you? You'll always gain more than you give, that I can promise you from experience.

# What Else Can You Do To Enhance Your Future?

## Public speaking

What a frightening proposal. I remember as a teenager, I considered getting up in front of a group as the nearest thing to hell that I could imagine. That was a feeling that didn't go away overnight.

*Heroes may not be braver than anyone else. They're just braver five minutes longer.*

**Ronald Reagan, Awarding Young American Medal for Bravery**

Am I seriously saying that you need public speaking experience to get a good job? Of course not. These are "nice to haves," not requirements. But how do you regard people who can stand up in front of a group and not only give a prepared presentation, but be assured enough to answer questions. How about speaking on a subject without even having any notes? Impossible? At your age, that may be the case.

But, if you ever expect to have a job where other people respect you and for which you're paid a satisfying salary, it's almost certain that you will sooner or later have to make presentations to others. That process starts with your very first job interview. The process may seem like a one-on-one conversation, but without any doubt, it's a presentation.

In my opinion, that set of circumstances is probably the best way to understand the nature of public speaking. The formal attempt to impart information orally to one person, or to 100 people, is nothing more than a one-sided conversation. In fact, a good presenter usually seems to be carrying on a two-sided conversation with the audience, whether the audience is responding out loud, or not.

I'll tell you why public speaking is so difficult. Few of us know enough about anything to be able to talk about it without notes and without planning exactly what we want to say. The nervousness we all feel is basically little more than uncertainty about the subject matter. The rest is just a matter of practice.

Even today, after years of teaching CPR with the Heart Association, how I feel in front of a group is dependent on how well I know my subject. I had to make a critically important presentation recently, and even though I knew the material well, the pressure in the days leading up to the presentation convinced me that I didn't. The night before the meeting, I think I slept a total of one hour. I was so nervous, my stomach was upset.

In the end, the fact that I really did know what I was talking about, and my years of experience in speaking to groups, got me through with flying colors. I enjoyed the presentation, and I actually looked forward to giving the presentation again the next day. Later, my bosses all told me how well I had done. That didn't hurt my reputation in the least!

*Every time I see something terrible, it's like I see it at age 19. I keep a freshness that way.*

**Ralph Nader,**
***Esquire***

Anyway, for you the goal is just to get started. You'd be surprised how easy it can be. While I can't write a book on public speaking for you right here in this chapter, I can suggest that you start small and make becoming comfortable in front of groups a lifetime challenge.

If you're serious about wanting to improve your speaking talents, there are no limits to the opportunities. In high school or in college, there are debate and forensic teams where you receive formal training and extensive practice in public speaking. If that's too intense for you, consider your activities or clubs. Could you volunteer to be an officer? Without having to give a formal presentation, you'll have numerous reasons to speak to the group.

No matter what avenue you choose, no matter how simple the approach may be, the more comfortable you become talking to people, the more self confident and the more socially respected you'll become. That result will help you in all aspects of your life.

## Tutoring/Mentoring

If public speaking is really only a one-sided conversation, and its purpose is to inform, then that sounds a lot like teaching. If you want to become more comfortable with putting your thoughts into spoken words, why not try tutoring? It's a great way to combine the two goals of volunteering and public speaking.

Again, all you really need is a subject which you know more about than someone else. There are probably a number of people your age who could use a bit of help in one or more subjects. If you're not aware who they are, let your school counselors know you're available. They'll know who needs the help.

It may be unusual in your circle of friends to tutor other people your age. No problem. Would you be willing to act as a mentor for a younger student? Elementary and middle school counselors are always looking for older people to tutor their students who have special needs. They really prefer older students, because the younger kids can identify with them so much more easily than with adults. Nothing will help your confidence and self image more than becoming a special person in someone else's eyes.

It's really easy to tutor a younger student in a subject you enjoyed yourself. It will, however, take some thorough planning and regular preparation. Furthermore, once you accept the responsibility, you're obligated to do your very best to fulfill your promises. Taking on that kind of job and succeeding in providing valuable assistance to another person will provide you with experience in planning, organizing, speaking, explaining, leading, and finishing what you start. What employer wouldn't love to have such proven talents in a potential employee?

*An optimist is a person who sees a green light everywhere, while the pessimist sees only the red stoplight. The truly wise person is colorblind.*

**Albert Schweitzer, *News Summaries***

## Working with the public

Another way to improve your speaking skills is to find a way to increase your interaction with the public. It's not necessary to be the center of attention in order to gain experience in communication. In fact, what I'm suggesting is pretty much in the opposite direction. I think it's helpful for a person to have had experience in serving the public.

Few things are more humbling than being in a position where your responsibility is to respond to other people's requests. It's sometimes a true test in patience to put up with the difficult people who run loose in this society. The types of jobs I'm thinking of are waiters, store clerks, receptionists, telephone operators, or service representatives.

Employers are finding it harder and harder to locate employees who can adhere to the motto, "the customer is always right." An applicant with experience in that area, especially one who truly has the maturity to appear to enjoy a service role, is probably worth his or her weight in gold. Have you ever had a summer job of that sort?

During my early years, I had a paper route, I bagged groceries, and I worked behind a counter selling bait and tackle at a fishing pier. Each job gave me numerous chances to deal with difficult people from a position where I had little control. Each job was definitely a learning experience.

What concrete value did I get from the experiences? Without any exaggeration, I can say that each of those experiences has been mentioned in an interview which produced comparable memories from the interviewer. I know I never made a point of bringing up such mundane jobs, but somehow one or the other often made its way into the conversation. Interviewers love to know what kind of early jobs people had while they were still in school.

As I've already said, employers have to find things that set applicants apart from each other. There are too many qualified people with the minimum necessary skills. Finding a person with experience in dealing with the public is a victory, even if the job doesn't require public contact. Evidence of success in dealing with difficult people is one of the most distinctive bonuses an applicant can offer.

*It's all that the young people can do for the old, to shock them and keep them up to date.*
**George Bernard Shaw,**
***Fanny's First Play***

If you think you have the patience to serve the public, consider such a summer or part-time job. As an alternative, you could choose a volunteer activity where dealing with people is your responsibility. Even in school, you could volunteer to be an office assistant or a teacher's assistant. Or how about an equipment manager or similar role for one of your sports teams at school? The opportunities are endless.

Find an opportunity that combines multiple advantages. Even a short-term effort (one summer, one semester, one evening per week for a month or two) will let you test your patience. It's possible that you may find you actually enjoy serving the public. Believe it or not, there are as many hidden gems out there as there are rotten apples.

## Personal relations — adult groups

When you apply for your first job, what type of person do you think is going to interview you? Who are you going to be reporting to and working with once you start that first job? Unless your experience is unusual, you're going to begin your career dealing with people quite a bit older than you. Are you prepared to communicate with them on their terms?

Again, we're talking here about respect, the essence of a service position. No matter how you feel about your boss or your co-workers, as the lowest on the ladder, you're going to be expected to show respect for your superiors and your elders. I'm sorry, I know you thought once parents and teachers were out of the way, you were free, but the respect thing just never ends. Until you're the top person in charge, you'll always report to someone else. Even the president of the company usually reports to a Board of Directors. And even the Board has to acknowledge the influence of the major stockholders.

You see, of course, where I'm heading. You need to be used to interacting with people older than your friends. You need to know how "older" people talk, how they act, how they think. You don't have to talk, act, or think like they do, but you do have to be able to fit into their world. How well prepared are you to interact smoothly with people ten to thirty years older than you?

*Ignorant people in preppy clothes are more dangerous to America than oil embargoes.*

**V. S. Naipul, professor at Wesleyan University, *Time***

There are a number of ways to improve your social mobility. It can be as simple as attempting to deal with your parents on a more mature, equal basis. OK, stop laughing, I know that's quite a stretch, but there is a bit of a lesson there, also. If you take away all the parent/offspring stresses that make that relationship so challenging, what's left is what you're going to face in the workplace. You will work with older people who think they know much more than you do and who have authority over you. It's certainly not fair to judge your potential for future success in the workplace by how well you get along with your parents, but you should at least acknowledge the similarities.

The better idea is to associate with a group that includes a significant number of older people. A group of people your age with one older leader is somewhat helpful, but I think a group with a majority of older people, or at least a mixed age group, is preferable. The goal is to see "maturity" in action. To be honest, you may be more mature (in the qualitative sense) than the members of the group, but you'll get a sense of what quantitative maturity implies.

The ideal is to spend time as a part of a group having an important purpose. Again, volunteer activities can supply that opportunity. In my experience, middle-aged people taking part in volunteer activities are as open, warm, and enjoyable as any people you're likely to meet. If you want a gentle introduction to working with people older than yourself, volunteer groups are a good bet. In addition, older people are usually so pleased to have young people express an interest in what they're doing that you'll probably get more personal attention and support than you would imagine.

Networking is an additional advantage in associating with an older age group. Throughout your career, you're going to find your best opportunities appear through connections with people you know. That may even have begun with your parents' assistance in finding your first job. The pattern will occur again and again. The more people you know who have the ability to assist you in life, the more assistance you'll find when you need it.

Yes, it's as simple as it sounds. If as a student, you make contacts with older people through a mutual interest, when the time comes to find a job, your sources for information on job openings will already be in place. If my company wanted to hire a high school student as a summer intern, where do you think I'd look for someone? I see fifty of those someones every Wednesday night at Junior Achievement. I'd hire any one of them in a moment. Get the picture? It works like that for any job, at any age, I promise.

## Politics

As strange as it may sound at your age, a great way to meet older people and make valuable, lasting contacts is through involvement in politics. I wouldn't be surprised to hear you say that you don't know anyone in politics and have no idea or opinion about any of the issues. No problem. Nobody's asking you to run for office, just to learn a little about the process.

Do you care at all about how your school system is run? Possibly your school board is an elected body. In many parts of the country, there are students serving on local school boards. At the very least, you can find out who your school board members are and determine how each of them view their responsibilities. If you're in general agreement with one of those individuals, why not work with them on their next campaign?

*Education is the ability to listen to almost anything without losing your temper or your self-confidence.*

**Robert Frost,**
***Reader's Digest***

Does your neighborhood have a citizen's association? Those groups are always looking for a young person to give them more insight into what's needed in the area. In my experience, those groups are always looking for help. If you have a computer and any skills in that area, they'll definitely find you something to do.

Even your local governing bodies, statewide representatives, and maybe even national political figures are not beyond your reach. Start small by asking for information about an issue that might interest you. Volunteer to stuff envelopes or deliver campaign circulars for a candidate during the next election. There are never enough people to run a campaign, and workers are always appreciated. You'll meet people who are influential in your community.

If you're old enough to vote, register and go to the polls whenever there's an issue to vote on or an office to fill. Once you're registered, you can volunteer to be a worker at a polling place on election day. Normally, you need to be registered as a Democrat or a Republican to be asked to be a poll watcher. If you're not sure which you prefer, just choose one. You can, of course, always vote for whomever you choose, and you can change your registration anytime you want.

During my several efforts as a poll watcher, I checked people's names against the authorized voting rolls, instructed them how to use voting machines, and counted vote totals at the end of the day for reporting to registrars. It was always a long day, but it was rewarding to know I was supporting the democratic system. I also met and worked with other people who became valuable contacts.

*Character consists of what you do on the third and fourth tries.*

**James Michener, *Chesapeake***

No matter what level of respect you may have for the American political system, your life is influenced daily by the decisions made within its structure. Even if your main purpose for getting involved is to make contacts or to become more comfortable in working with older people, the lessons you learn by working in the political arena will serve you well throughout the rest of your life.

## Sales Experience/Fundraising

Another avenue for testing your maturity level, and for developing talents of value to future employers, involves learning how to ask people for money. It may sound like a rather harsh way to phrase the subject of this section, but that's really the essence of selling or soliciting charitable contributions.

It doesn't matter whether you ever anticipate a career in sales, or not, acquiring the confidence and poise to look a person in the eyes and ask for some of their hard earned cash is a significant achievement. In spite of that, for the majority of people, it's not an attractive concept. If you dislike being asked for money, it's only natural to recoil from the idea of having to be the one doing the asking.

As a young person, I, too, hated sales. During the time I had my paper route, the newspaper sponsored periodic sales contests. I never did very well going door to door trying to add subscribers. The same held true for candy and doughnut sales by the school band. I hated the idea, so I didn't put too much effort into it. I've found out since that working harder would have been worth the effort.

I learned that fact ten years ago when my employer one day decided to "loan" me to the local United Way Campaign. In many cities, employers make a contribution to the campaign by sending one or more employees to work full-time with the United Way Campaign for three to four months. The employer continues to pay the salary while the United Way gets the benefit of the labor. The Loaned Executive helps companies conduct their own fundraising campaigns.

I was chosen because I had been a volunteer company United Way campaign coordinator many times, and I did have public speaking experience. It was a great "honor," and I was completely "thrilled." Actually, in the end, it was a great experience, and three years later, I volunteered to do it again. However, in the beginning it was a frightening challenge.

*The most important function of education at any level is to develop the personality of the individual and the significance of his life to himself and to others. This is the basic architecture of a life. The rest is ornamentation and decoration of the structure.*

**Grayson Kirk, President, Columbia University, *Quote***

My job was to contact the decision-makers in major companies and convince them to establish (or help them continue) their own in-company campaigns. Much of that persuasion was carried out over the telephone. Each day for several weeks, I sat in a room with twenty-three other people making those telephone calls. I sure could have profited from earlier experience in selling a product and in selling myself.

Then I had to help company coordinators plan their campaigns, and I participated in fundraising presentations to company employees. During my first several months, I spoke to groups as large as 250 people, asking them to give money to the United Way. It was difficult at first, not so much the public speaking part but deciding the most appropriate way to ask people to open their wallets.

Once the job was done and I was back working on my regular duties, I began to see the value of what I had learned. My job at that time involved developing and implementing compensation plans for insurance agents. Few occupations involve more complicated pay schemes than insurance, and the agents were always confused and usually frustrated about the way they got paid. I spent as much time explaining the rules and "selling" them on the fairness of the system as I did managing the numbers that were involved. After the experience I'd gained in helping people to understand the intangible benefits of donating money, it was a lot easier to understand how to communicate the tangible aspects of a compensation scheme to a true salesman.

While not a salesman myself, my job required an understanding of the sales thought process. It's as basic as the need to be able to communicate to another person how the product or service you or your company offers is worth more than the cost to the consumer. You'll find that a large percentage of jobs are based more on sales expertise than you might have expected.

Furthermore, when you realize that you sell yourself every day to people who can reward you in very tangible ways, you'll see that you are a salesperson at every stage of your life. The more experience you develop at selling or encouraging people to contribute money, the more valuable you'll be to an employer, and the more effective you'll be at producing benefits for yourself.

If you're at all interested in the concept, fundraising opportunities are endless. If any of your activities involve organizations that need to raise funds, you've probably already tried to avoid requests to help solicit donations. Next time, just say "yes." If you're not already involved in a group, the next time some charitable group has a walk-a-thon or a bowl-a-thon or whatever they do to raise pledges, get involved. If you've never gone door-to-door, you've got to try it at least once.

I'm proud to be providing such experience to my Junior Achievement students. They learn how to sell products. Sure, they mostly convince their parents and friends to buy the things they sell, but some of them take the effort really seriously. The program encourages the door-to-door effort, and some of them have made twenty or more sales. There you have your successful business people of the future.

## Reading and Writing

If it sounds like I'm covering the basics again, don't be surprised. These days, employers are thrilled to find applicants well-grounded in the basic skills of reading and writing. Those abilities are rare enough, even at my level. I'm usually referred to in my department as "the staff writer." That's not because no one else writes well; it's because I do write well and I've built a reputation for being someone who enjoys writing. Whenever an important paper needs to be written, I usually get to do at least the first draft.

Helping you to give an employer a reason to think of you first when a job needs to get done is why I wrote this book. The ability to read complicated material, understand all the implications of what you've read, and organize your thoughts on paper is far and away one of the most valuable talents you can offer an employer.

Learning to write well, like acquiring most important talents, is not an overnight process. I wasn't a particularly good writer in high school, either. Would you like to know the greatest advantage I had in learning to write? I was an avid reader. During my earliest years my parents read to me all the time. As soon as I could read for myself, I became addicted to comic books. I soon graduated to science fiction. Along the way, I made frequent side trips into historical fiction, international spy thrillers, detective stories, Stephen King, and in recent years, a good bit of modern philosophy.

*Reading is a means of thinking with another person's mind; it forces you to stretch your own.*
**Charles Scribner, Jr.,**
***Publisher's Weekly***

As you can see, it wasn't always intellectual stuff. My opinion is that almost any reading is helpful to the development of your ability to write. You can't read extensively without beginning to think in more literary phrases. I don't believe your actual speech patterns will change much, although your vocabulary will increase dramatically. The importance is that when you do have to write something, you'll know inherently whether what you're putting on paper sounds like the things you've been reading. By itself, that won't make your writing better, but it will make you aware of your progress.

The most important tool I found in learning to enjoy writing was the personal computer. I hated writing longhand. My handwriting wasn't attractive, it made my hand hurt, and I could never get a thought down on paper fast enough. It was in college when I finally began to realize that I needed to know how to type. Papers had to be turned in typed, and I didn't have the time or the money to have someone else transcribe my handwritten work.

I have to admit I learned by the "hunt and peck" process, and I'm still not a touch typist, but I can now type at least thirty words per minute which is quite acceptable. If you ever have the chance to learn typing the correct way, it will be worth more to you over the years than I can begin to explain.

Once you know how to type and you have access to a computer, you have to learn word processing. The word sounds intimidating, but it's so simple, I'd be ashamed of you if you were hesitant to learn it as soon as you could. Once every sentence you write can be corrected, moved, copied, rearranged, saved, and printed in split seconds, you're nearly the master of language.

Once the manual effort of writing is minimized, you can concentrate on making your words effective. It's like going to the foul line in a basketball game and being told you can shoot until you make the basket. Sure, you have to understand what the goal is, and you have to have the ability to throw the ball far enough, but beyond that, you're home free.

With effort, patience, and time, the personal computer with word processing software has made it possible for nearly everyone to write reasonably well. All it takes is practice. To an extent, the challenge is the same as public speaking, but without the pressure. The most important step is to have something to say. I won't minimize that challenge, but the point of being one of the "best and brightest" and having an expectation of future success is the assumption that you do have a lot of knowledge and ability. You do have things to say, or at least you have the power to find things to say with a little effort.

*If you see the magic in a fairy tale, you can face the future.*

**Danielle Steel, *Family Album***

In today's society, it seems like only the "writers" do any writing. My proposition to you is that you better become one of those writers. In a world becoming more and more complex, the winners of the future are going to be the people who can explain the world to everyone else. That's going to happen through public speaking or private writing. You can have your choice, but you better develop your talents at one of them.

If you need suggestions for where to start, again there are numerous ways. Do you ever write letters to anyone? If not, please write a long letter to your mother, grandmother, or whoever you feel guilty about not having written to in a long time. You know there's someone. No more valuable, but more likely to occur, put some extra effort into your next paper for school. Instead of writing for the teacher or for the grade, imagine that you're writing an article to go in a textbook on the subject. If you were teaching the course, would the paper you're writing be a helpful teaching aid? Someday your writing at work will be assessed for how well it communicates to others, so you better practice some self-assessment now.

The ideal approach would be to try writing a letter to an editor about a subject or an event that interests you. Write an article for the school newspaper. You don't have to be on the staff of the paper to do that. Write something for one of your clubs. They always need promotional material or a basic guidebook to the operations and goals of the organization.

I have to warn you not to be disappointed if no one encourages you or if you can't seem to get anything published. The point is to work on your writing. Personally, I think if you work at it, and if your expectations are reasonable, you will eventually see some of your writing in print. What's more valuable, though, is the progress you'll be making toward the day when you can tell a prospective employer, "Oh, yes, I think I write fairly well, and I enjoy writing. If you hire me, I'll be glad to help whenever papers or reports need to be written." Want to stand out from the crowd? That'll do it!

## Personal Growth

To be honest, this topic is more the subject of the next part of the book. However, even in this part, which concentrates on things you can do while you're still in school to prepare for life "after," I do want to mention the importance of personal growth in areas beyond specific job skills. Think of it as an introduction to the sections that lie ahead.

In my opinion, your basic goal in preparing yourself for the future is to become the best you can be at whatever will help you to function as a talented, mature, employable, and happy adult. With the priority of finding rewarding, enjoyable employment as the focus of this book so far, I've tried to point out all the many talents that will aid you in that pursuit.

The final areas to consider while you're still in school are the things you can do to become a more interesting individual in a personal sense. Obviously, an employer will be looking for specific talents that will make you valuable in getting the work completed. Less obviously, even less consciously, he or she will be looking for traits that will make you a pleasant person to work with. Everything you can do to be an attractive person socially will pay dividends in addition to your potential value as a worker.

At this point, I'm speaking only of the continual effort to widen your range of interests. Just as each past work and school experience will have relevance to some employer sooner or later, your personal interests also have potential for making you "special" in some employer's eyes. The greater benefit is that the more things you truly enjoy in life, the happier you will undoubtedly be. If one of your interests happens to coincide with an employer's, it's a wonderfully fortunate coincidence.

There's really little need to spend time on examples. Like my recommendations to get involved in activities or volunteer organizations, I think you should find a source of entertainment, a hobby, or a challenge that you

enjoy, and that makes you a more interesting person. I don't care whether it's art, music, dancing, ski-jumping, civil war reenactments, or professional wrestling. Somebody, somewhere will find that pursuit makes you a special person. If, at the same time, that interest has enhanced your own satisfaction with life, you've accomplished two very important goals.

I told you at the beginning of this section of the book that my goal was to reduce the stress you, a high school student, are probably feeling. One last stress probably needs to be addressed, one that I actually may have heightened myself. This section of the book has discussed many, many ways to improve your background, make you more attractive to potential employers, and I hope, help you to become more satisfied with yourself. What I have risked doing is establishing a measure of success that is, at the least, quite overwhelming.

Early in the first section of this book, I warned you about comparing yourself to others. Now is a good time to repeat that warning. You've just finished reading about all the things that may make you a happier, more "attractive" person. How many of you are ready to go out tomorrow and begin trying to accomplish them all? Wrong!! That's not the way to find happiness, or to become a more attractive person. That's the way to dump so much stress on yourself that you become a frustrated, unhappy, potentially quite unlikable person.

*How many cares one loses when one decides not to be something, but to be someone.*

**Gabrielle ("Coco") Chanel, *This Week***

You are already a wonder of creation as you sit there today reading these words. Your accomplishments to this point in your life and your desire to be even "better" than you are now should make you feel as "attractive" as many people could ever hope to imagine. No, I don't expect you're as happy with yourself as you want to be. Few people are, and few ever will be as satisfied as they think they should be. Your advantage is that you're young, you're talented, you have the opportunities to get ahead, and in spite of your youthful impatience, you have all the time you need.

If you want to go out tomorrow and start a new project to enhance your life, that's beautiful. I'll feel I've done you a service to have motivated you to such action. If you feel you need to become a completely different person by next week, next month, or next year, you scare me. Life, to me, is a series of daily baby steps, from those first staggering lunges across the living room floor, to the small smile of realization at a much later age that you like yourself a little more today than you did yesterday.

*The tragedy of life doesn't lie in not reaching your goal. The tragedy lies in having no goal to reach.*

**Benjamin E. Mays, President, Morehouse College,** ***NY Times***

If you want to begin the progress toward liking yourself better, take a little baby step tomorrow and read an interesting book. Take another one next week by volunteering at a library or a nursing home. Take one next semester by registering for a course in a subject you never would have considered before, one that will send your growth in another interesting direction. A year from now, stop and count the steps you've taken and decide if you like yourself better. That's the time frame for realistic measurements. Go easy on yourself and celebrate the small steps for what they are, part of a lifetime of learning to walk. It's a long journey into a fascinating future. "One small step" at a time is all it takes to succeed.

*My job is to bore you and let the hardness of your seat and the warmth of your robe prepare you for what is to come.*

**William H. McNeil, Professor of History, Univ. Of Chicago, Commencement address at Bard College**

# Chapter 6

## The First Job

Now you know more about what employers want. I hope you're beginning to see that what you're learning in high school, and what you expect to accomplish in college, will make a difference in your future success. Before we move on to a review of your college selection process, let's look at one other aspect of "what employers want."

## Life in Your First Job

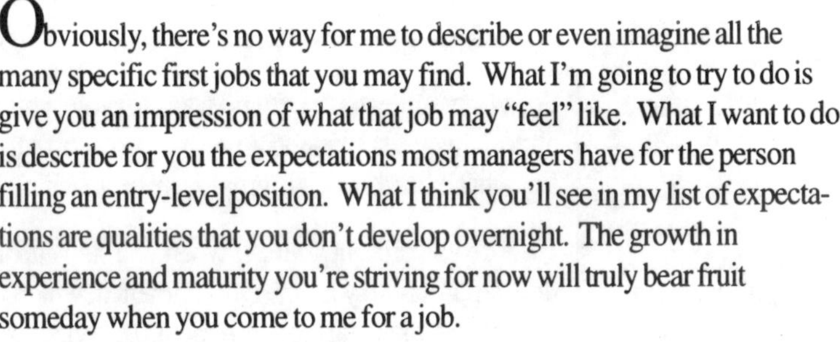

Obviously, there's no way for me to describe or even imagine all the many specific first jobs that you may find. What I'm going to try to do is give you an impression of what that job may "feel" like. What I want to do is describe for you the expectations most managers have for the person filling an entry-level position. What I think you'll see in my list of expectations are qualities that you don't develop overnight. The growth in experience and maturity you're striving for now will truly bear fruit someday when you come to me for a job.

You'll find there aren't a lot of ways to prove yourself in entry-level jobs. The biggest desire supervisors have in relation to entry-level employees is dependability. Are you someone who virtually always gets where you're going on time? Do you have to be really sick before you cancel something you've promised to do? Do you have the concentration to work on a project for at least an hour without having to take a break? For some people, those simple standards are easily attained; for others they seem completely impossible.

Place those expectations in a work environment and they reflect the primary expectations you'll face in your first permanent job. Some employers look at punctuality, attendance, and total concentration on the job as inviolable rules ... one lapse and you're out. In those situations, you're in big trouble. Most employers, however, realize that you are human. Your car is going to break down, you are going to get sick, you do have to go to the bathroom once in a while.

Even the most sympathetic employers, however, will watch you very carefully during the first months on the job. This scrutiny will feel unfair, and you're likely to think they're picking on you more than on others. It may be true, because they consider you to be in the process of proving yourself. If you can't show dependability in a brand new job at the beginning, they sure won't expect you to get better with time. The new kid on the block is always watched more carefully. Expect it, and don't let it get to you. An opportunity to "prove yourself" is a privilege; at least that's how employers see it. I do, too.

If you want to make a success of your first job, you'll have to consider adopting an approach that will serve you well in all parts of your life. "Give 'em even better than they expect!" It should never be considered demeaning to try to impress someone by trying harder than anyone else. I understand that sometimes peer pressure not to overdo it can be restrictive. No one liked the "curve breaker" in school. But in the real world, you have the simple choice never to move ahead, or to consider giving just a little bit extra. That's a habit you can start working on right away.

*Only the curious will learn and only the resolute overcome the obstacles to learning. The quest quotient has always excited me more than the intelligence quotient.*

**Eugene S. Wilson, Dean of Admissions, Amherst College, *Reader's Digest***

So, let's assume you've found ways to prove you're dependable. You're almost always at work on time, and you don't miss days on a regular basis. For what other things will employers be watching?

How do you present yourself when you show up in the morning? Do you dress appropriately for the environment in which you work? Your job is not the place to make fashion statements by trying to stand out from everyone else. Someday, wearing something outlandish once in a while will be appreciated for the diversion it makes, but as a new employee, your job is to conform. Sorry, that's the way it works.

How do you get along with your co-workers? Even if they're a bunch of uptight old *****s, can you deal with them and get your work finished? What the boss will be watching for are your efforts to do just that. Can you fit into both worlds? Can you become a part of your co-workers' group, while still trying to show your special talents and differences? Walking a tightrope is a difficult and sometimes dangerous endeavor, but accomplishing it proves a lot to everyone still standing on the ground.

Bottom line: supervisors are human, and they like to be around pleasant people. The work environment can be, and usually is, one of the most stressful places on earth. Anyone who makes it less stressful becomes a valuable person. I hope you've found that's true in high school, too.

Does all this make employers seem like harsh, demanding taskmasters? Are you tempted to think of them as unfair? Employers consider your first job a beginning, a chance for you to prove to them, and even to yourself, that you're as dependable and as strong as any new graduate can be. The reason their view of you may seem impersonal is that at work they usually have to see you as a resource first and a person second.

If you can ignore the hard implications of that for a moment, think about the situation logically. To any large organization you work for, you're likely to be a very small part of the overall operation. It's impossible for everyone in a large organization to be concerned on a personal level with everyone else. Your value comes from whether or not you give more to the organization than you take.

Think about that concept for a moment. Many people seem to evaluate themselves on the basis of whether they "do what they're paid to do." Or they may phrase it in terms of wanting the organization to "pay them for what they do." In most organizations, and certainly in a capitalistic society, businesses are expected to make a profit. That means they're supposed to provide a product or a service to customers at a price which is higher than the organization's own cost of production. In other words, they have to create efficiencies of production in which they pay less for raw materials and production costs than the value of what they produce.

*The society that scorns excellence in plumbing because plumbing is a humble activity, and tolerates shoddiness in philosophy because philosophy is an exalted activity, will have neither good plumbing nor good philosophy. Neither its pipes nor its theories will hold water.*

**John W. Gardiner, President, Carnegie Foundation, *Saturday Evening Post***

Do you hear what that implies? The essence of capitalism, by that thought process, is the payment to employees of less than they're worth. So you see, it's not a conspiracy to rip off the workers when they're paid less than they think they deserve, it's the primary goal of the people who run the organizations.

That's heavy, isn't it? No, I'm not really trying to defend slave wages while companies make millions, but I want you to consider seriously what your value will be to an organization in your first job. Will you be willing to give more value to the organization than the amount of money you're being paid? Very few people realize that is their goal, at least from the point of view of the organization. When you're in your first job and are trying to build a future for yourself, it's the concept of giving more than is expected that will move you along faster than someone else.

When your time comes, and it will, plan to begin your career by being the best that you can be. Deciding to treat your job that way and learning to live that way in all aspects of your life are the first steps to success and happiness. That approach to life can start right now. If it hasn't, why wait any longer?

## A First Job Summary

Welcome back to the present. Yes, you're back in high school again (sorry about that). What did you think of your first job? Actually, I didn't tell you much about the job itself, did I? Like I said, the specifics of each job are so different, it really would have been impossible to describe the duties of an "average" first job.

What I hope I've been able to do is to give you a first impression of the employers you'll face and the workplace you'll enter once you leave school. It really will be like taking off the training wheels. The supports you've always depended on — parents, friends, counselors — will all be further away. They won't be gone; it's just that you finally will have entered the world of a responsible adult.

It's where you've wanted to be for all the years you can remember ... on your own ... free to design your life the way you want it to be. No matter how difficult the challenges, they someday will actually be under your own control. I guess I should warn you that it won't feel like the simple, joyful accomplishment you thought it would be. I can promise you, however, that it will offer all the rewards you can imagine if you're ready to take the difficult challenges as no more than exciting opportunities.

*Life is not having been told that the man has just waxed the floor.*

**Ogden Nash,**
***You and Me and P. B. Shelley***

Since you're still in school full-time and probably haven't experienced the final freedom of being totally responsible for yourself, you may not be able to appreciate the magnitude of that challenge quite yet. To give you a perspective for what lies ahead at that stage of your life, a later section of this book will talk about your first year out of school. I do believe that you'll be better off if you read it before you get there. Little you do at twenty-one will be unfixable later, but everything you do then and now will provide resources for who you are and what you have later.

*Twenty Years of Schoolin' / And they put you on the day shift.*

**Bob Dylan, "Subterranean Homesick Blues"**

That's been my point all along, hasn't it? What you're doing right now has great relevance to what you'll face later. Remember, I didn't say what you do now will determine what happens to you later, only that understanding the future, and making good use of the present, can make your path easier and a lot more pleasant.

With that perspective you're now ready to get back to the decision that represents your immediate concern. How does your improved view of the future influence how you choose a college? It's an exciting prospect, isn't it? This next section will help.

*It is always wise to look ahead, but difficult to look farther than you can see.*

**Winston S. Churchill, *Observer***

# Chapter 7

## I Want It All!

Remember my college friend Michele? What do you think her primary concern was when she and I began talking? "Am I going to be able to get that perfect job when I graduate?" Maybe she didn't phrase it quite that way, but that's what she was thinking. She even mentioned the rumors of the $35,000 — $40,000 starting pay jobs that you could get if you had all the right credentials.

Do those jobs exist? I guess they do, but my reaction is, "Do people win a million dollars in the lottery?" Sure they do, but the odds are several million to one against winning. Even more interesting, are those million dollar winners happier than everyone else? They sure are for a while, I won't deny that, but how about later? I haven't gotten the impression that the majority of them end up any happier than I am. So do you have a really good chance of finding one of those sensational jobs right out of college, and will you only be happy if you do find one?

I truly hope you didn't answer "yes" to either part of that question. If you did, I'm not sure I'm the best one to help you. If you're at least willing to consider a "no" answer for both parts of the question, then we can talk sensibly about what most of you will face in searching for and finding your first job.

We should at least acknowledge the most attractive possibilities. I do believe in setting your sights high. If you can't imagine unlimited success, you'll probably never even attain realistic success. Yes, there are some really super jobs out there. They usually involve being in just the right field, at just the right time, in just the right place, if you're willing to be just the person an organization wants you to be. There are an awful lot of "justs" in those requirements, some of which can cost you a lot, "just" to make that big salary.

One of the big problems is that choosing a field to prepare for is a delicate proposition. A formal education in a technical field can take anywhere from a 2-3 to a 4-8 year commitment. What's "hot" today may be "cold" two years from now, or by then there may be five million other new graduates who made the same choice and are now competing for one million jobs in the field. Not great odds.

For instance, I read in an issue of *Kiplinger's Personal Finance* magazine that for 1995 graduates, starting salaries of chemical engineers ($40,000) and computer programmers ($32,000) were among the top opportunities. If you're about to start college now, by the time you finish, the data above will be six or seven years old. Sure, you'll get new data as you go along, but are you going to switch majors each time a new set of studies is issued? It's going to be very difficult to chase the top dollars with that kind of time horizon.

*We all want to be famous people and the moment we want to be something, we are no longer free.*

**Krishnamurti,**
***The Penguin Krishnamurti Reader***

Bureau of Labor Statistics research does highlight a number of points that are important. First, a college degree is still the ticket to future job opportunities. Of the top 10 percent of wage earners in 1990, more than 82 percent had college experience. Second, in spite of all you hear about managerial layoffs, in the last fifteen years, growth in the number of management jobs has been 83 percent, compared to overall job growth of only 37 percent. And third, growth in the number of higher paying jobs over the last eighteen years (jobs paying more than $50,000 - up 117 percent; jobs paying more than $75,000 - up 145 percent, both adjusted for inflation) has far exceeded all job growth (an increase of 58 percent).

All that really says is that if you're making plans to go to college, you're already working toward accomplishing the most important thing you can do to create opportunities for a satisfying and well-paying future job. But still, I hear you saying, what do you choose to study now to increase your chances of success?

## College — The Big Question

As I've already stated, if you're reading this book, I assume you're a highly motivated, talented, fairly successful high school student ... one of the "best and the brightest." If you've not already committed yourself to going to college, you're pretty sure that it's what you expect to do. Your question is not, "Is college a good idea?" It's more about what the college experience is meant to be.

It's the question that led to this book, and the one that probably tops your list if you already understand that the purpose of college is to prepare you for the future. "Why do I really want to go to college, and what should I do with the opportunity?" College will be fun, and it'll certainly be exciting, but it also better teach you something you can use once you've finished. That means you better make a college choice based on some assurance that you'll learn something worthwhile.

College is intended to prepare you to seek your own successful, satisfying place in society. Among the many aspects of that goal is the expectation that you'll want to develop skills which will enable you to get a job and support yourself. Every job requires basic, specific skills that you can usually be taught in school. It's impossible to deny that access to most good jobs is dependent on having the educational background needed to do, or at least to learn the job. If you want to be an accountant, you need to study accounting; if you want to program computers, you need to study computer programming.

So how should a high school student go about contemplating the future, or to be more specific, choosing a college to attend after high school? A discussion of what the student might like to do in the future is a logical start. A review of job opportunities is a relevant step in establishing a frame of reference for such important decisions.

## Jobs of the Future

The U.S. Bureau of Labor Statistics continually attempts to provide data helpful in "predicting" the future. As summarized by Carol Kleinman in a *Chicago Tribune* article, the Bureau has issued its 1995 biennial projections for job changes through the year 2005. In the goods-producing sector, only construction will add any significant number of jobs. Manufacturing will continue to decline but will still account for one out of seven jobs.

As we would all expect, the job growth will be in the service industries. The services and retail trade industries will account for 16.2 million out of a total projected growth of 16.8 million wage and salary jobs. Health care services will account for almost one-fifth of all job growth from 1994 to 2005. The personnel services industry, which provides temporary help to employers in other industries, is projected to add 1.3 million jobs. Temporary workers tend to have low wages, low job stability, and poor job benefits.

*The word 'liberal' distinguishes whatever nourishes the mind and spirit from the training which is merely practical or professional or from the trivialities which are no training at all.*

**Alan Simpson, President, Vassar College, Address at 100th Commencement**

Employment in professional specialty occupations is projected to increase at a faster rate than any other major occupational group. Employment of computer engineers and systems analysts is expected to grow rapidly.

Health services is the fastest expanding industry, with a projected job growth of 84 percent. Residential care will grow by 83 percent, computer and data-processing services by 69 percent, social services by 69 percent, and business services by 68 percent. Business services are represented by companies providing such things as legal services, mail services and marketing to companies that have decided to buy rather than create such things for themselves. The next five fastest growing industries are child care services, personnel supply services, building services, equipment leasing, and public relations.

As far as occupations go, the top five fastest growing are personal and home care aides with 119 percent growth, home health aides with 102 percent, systems analysts with 92 percent, computer engineers with 90 percent, and physical therapists' assistants with 83 percent. Included among the remaining top 20 are physical therapists, paralegals, and teachers.

First place in number of new hires will be cashiers, adding 562,000 jobs, followed by janitors and cleaners adding 559,000, retail salespersons adding 532,000, waiters and waitresses adding 479,000, registered nurses adding 473,000, general managers and top executives adding 466,000, systems analysts adding 445,000, home health aides adding 428,000, guards adding 415,000, nursing aides and orderlies adding 387,000, and secondary school teachers adding 386,000.

As pointed out in Ms. Kleinman's article, the statistics show job creation at the two ends of the spectrum—professional jobs and low-wage jobs. What's missing are the middle-range jobs. Some might find that conclusion worrisome to today's students, but I don't think it's all bad news. Let's take a look at what I see as the positives.

First is the continued creation of technical jobs. Occupations which require a bachelor's degree or above will average 23 percent growth, almost double the 12 percent growth projected for occupations requiring less education and training. There appears to be good reason to anticipate access to jobs where advanced training (read college training) is needed.

If you're a technically-oriented person with interests in computers, business, health, or the sciences (especially the environment), there should be multiple alternatives for you to consider.

Next is the incredible growth expected in the health services and the personal services fields. If you're a people-oriented person who likes working with and helping others, you'll find no lack of people needing your help. While many health careers can involve years of specialized study beyond four year programs, it also appears that the majority of the new positions will require much less of such postgraduate study, yet will offer higher than average earnings. It's likely that two-year special programs, and maybe even specializations during regular four-year programs, will be sufficient to enable you to find satisfying employment straight out of college.

Even the large growth in low-paying jobs may present some interesting positive opportunities. The nature of low wage jobs is usually that the person in the job is not expected to be able to make business decisions, solicit new business, or supervise other workers. As the number of these jobs increases, resulting, I have to assume, from a need for the services these jobs provide, the number of people needed to supervise these jobs will also increase.

*The basic purpose of a liberal arts education is to liberate the human being to exercise his or her potential to the fullest.*

**Barbara M. White, President, Mills College, *Christian Science Monitor***

While it may not take a college-educated person to supervise low-wage workers, competition for supervisor jobs will likely lead to college training as an advantage. Someone needs to help manage service companies, and the services these companies offer have to be marketed to the public. For that matter, if the demand for those services is there, someone has to create the new competitive companies who will create these new jobs. It doesn't take a college education to create a company, either, but the background acquired there makes a big difference in understanding what it takes to make a company succeed.

My point is that the statistics have a positive slant. An educated, ambitious young person in the years ahead will have opportunities. Predicting exactly what each opportunity will be is impossible. Preparing to take advantage of whatever opportunities may arise is not.

# Contemplating a Career Choice

Unfortunately, that brings us back to what I discussed previously. How do you predict four years, or even two years in advance which fields will be the highest paying and most in demand when your turn comes to find a job? This chapter will help you decide whether that's truly the right question to ask.

The "career choice" question is often asked as early as freshmen year in high school. Since you're currently in high school, either already making specific choices among colleges, or only reasonably certain that higher education is in your plans, it's important for you to understand what you're actually trying to accomplish. Usually, you're asked what you want to do after you graduate from college, and then you're matched up with a school that has a good program in that area.

*It is not enough to offer a smorgasbord of courses. We must insure that students are not just eating at one end of the table.*

**A. Bartlett Giamatti, President Yale Univ., "The American Teacher," *Harper's***

Assuming all the other factors involved in a college choice are acceptable (cost, location, size, etc.), it's not an inappropriate approach. However, I'd like to suggest a slightly different slant, at least in terms of the implications of the analysis.

Are you willing to acknowledge the significant likelihood that your career orientation at age forty will be different from what you think it will be at the moment? If you're not sure, ask your parents to do a quick survey of their friends. How many are now in jobs that match their high school expectations? How many even had the same job goals when they graduated from college that they had before they started? Unless you're different from the norm, you'll go through many changes in what you want to do as your life's work. Do you really want to make your college choice based on a desire that will likely change as you grow and mature?

OK, I'll admit the obvious, you do have to start somewhere. The best place to start is an analysis of what you think you might like to do. Some people are very sure what they want. If you feel that way, go for it! Even if your preference is only a general leaning in a certain direction, at least it's a direction. I wouldn't begin to suggest that you ignore it.

The point I'm approaching, however slowly, is that I feel you have an obligation to yourself to take a wide view of what lies ahead in your life. How are you going to feel if, in your sophomore year at a business school, you find that you really don't like business and finance? What if after three years of a pre-med program, you realize you can't stand the idea of being a doctor? Are you prepared for such a realization? Do you know what you'll do then?

So what does the "wide view of what lies ahead" mean? Are you not supposed to choose because the choice might change? Not at all, in fact, the number one point of this entire book is going to be stated in the next sentence.

You are going to change directions time and time again throughout your entire life; if you can accept that now and begin to plan for how to handle those decision points, life will become much more exciting and much less intimidating.

There, that wasn't so painful, was it? Making a choice about what college to attend and what course of study to pursue is one of the most important decisions you will make during your teenage years. Is the decision binding? No. Will you have other opportunities to change your decision? Yes. Is that simple enough?

If you think you have a good idea of what interests you and what program you'd like to begin with in college, there's no better place to start than at a school where you can receive such training. What I believe is that you should try to find a school where you can receive that training while still having the opportunity to accumulate a wide, diverse background in many different areas.

Once upon a time, that was the basic purpose of a college education. Young people were given the widest possible exposure to the knowledge of the world with the intention that they become "learned individuals," prepared to address whatever challenges they might face. Then the age of specialization came upon us. Every job was unique. Each discipline was so technically complex that only those indoctrinated in its most secret rituals could dare to trod the sacred path. All hail the mighty MBA. Let not any common mortal presume to understand the workings of the world.

If those words are not already totally ridiculous, even to you at your early age, let me assure you that managers today are also coming to realize the absurdity surrounding the myth of the magically empowered specialized degree. Too many narrowly educated specialists these days are entering the work force unable to write a simple letter, incapable of understanding the dynamics of the workplace, and unable to see a perspective larger than the formulas they were taught in college. Four years of concentration in a technical discipline have produced workers technically astute but practically unprepared for the real world.

Overstated? Maybe a little. But what do I, as a business executive who often hires people into their first jobs, look for in a college graduate these days?

Do you remember the things I listed as attractive additions to a resume, such as the skills of writing and speaking? How about mathematics, history, economics, languages, and geography? *U.S. News & World Report*'s "America's Best Colleges" issue confirms my beliefs. The Report notes, "Students are also discovering that many corporate employers have embraced the wisdom of educators who, even during the business boom, continued to preach the value of a liberal arts education."

The political implications of the word "liberal," and the music/dance/painting connotation of the word "art," certainly don't make you think about a way to prepare for a well-paying job. In spite of that, schools with strong liberal arts programs are making a comeback. And even business schools are starting to acknowledge the need to provide students with a wider background. Recently, the AASCB (the business school trade organization) began requiring that at least 50 percent of a business major's classes be in non-business classes, up from the 40 percent standard established 70 years ago.

*For I don't care too much for money, / For money can't buy me love.*

**John Lennon and Paul McCartney, "Can't Buy Me Love"**

If you want to preserve your greatest number of career options during the years you spend in college and prepare yourself ahead of time for the inevitable changes that will occur in the workplace, why not build the widest, most versatile background possible? There's nothing wrong with spending the first year or two of your college career taking lots of different types of courses. Sure, you can take one or two courses each semester in the specific area that interests you most, but don't brush off the value of the English, history, foreign language, or philosophy courses.

And even if your course of study is already in one of those areas, don't ignore the opportunity to take some math, biology, or business courses. Not only will you gain new perspectives on your field of concentration, you may find you really do have other interests that deserve further investigation.

I sometimes wonder if many people have a subconscious fear of finding they harbor wide ranging interests. It can be quite comforting to choose a narrow path and concentrate hard, not wavering in the least. It's also quite easy to remember parental criticisms of "not being able to finish one project before starting on another." And who hasn't heard the stories of poor souls described as "jack of all trades, master of none?"

To be honest, it's the nature of youth to change interests rapidly and indiscriminately. That's part of growing up and learning what's right and wrong, what's worth doing and what's not. On the other hand, one important measure of maturity is being able to do more than one thing at once. It's a trait critically needed in our complicated world and sorely lacking in many casualties of the workplace. A student who finds he or she has many interests and can enjoyably investigate them all before choosing to concentrate in one will be a better prepared employee in many ways, both in their educational background and in their maturity.

The "master of none" fallacy is another misleading complaint. The first section of this book has already noted the lack of technical challenge likely in a first job. Mastery is not the goal at that stage. The goal is to get that first job, to perform admirably, and to continue to learn as much as possible. It's true that you have to prepare for "a job," and that means choosing a field, taking the right courses, and presenting yourself as ready for the work. Don't, however, think you can disregard the jacks of all trades. They're the ones who somehow always seem qualified to compete with you for the next job opening. And, just as important, I'll contend that they're the ones who always seem just a bit more confident and a little more self-satisfied than most everyone else. Don't you think that may be important, if what we're really talking about here is being happy?

To put it as simply as possible, if you have a strong interest, pursue it ambitiously, but don't focus too narrowly. You might regret it later. If you're not sure what you want to do, don't be afraid to consider beginning college with the old, traditional liberal arts approach. Give yourself a year or two to "see the world" in an educational sense. There's still plenty of time to prepare for that one, specific, rewarding first job. Develop yourself first. The job prospects will, to a very great extent, develop right along with you.

*There is no more vulnerable human combination than an undergraduate.*

**John Sloan Dickey, President, Dartmouth, *The Atlantic***

# Chapter 8

## Getting Into Your College of Choice—A Mutual Selection

Let me guess. No matter what you now think about choosing a college, you're still unsure whether you can get in the school you want. I'll be more direct. Are you fearful that your grades and SAT scores aren't good enough to make a college want you? If you feel that way, join the crowd. *The Washington Post* reported that even Chelsea Clinton thought she needed an SAT Prep course to improve her chances of being selected. This chapter is intended to reduce the stress you feel about college admissions. One good place to start is a discussion about your grades.

At every age from high school freshman to graduate student, there seems to be someone who will tell you that your grades are critical to your future. You, the current best and brightest, you believe those warnings, don't you? You're convinced that each "A" is a rung on the ladder, and each "B" a failure. You suffer during each test, and you can almost get physically ill when you hear the words, "pop quiz," can't you?

You, personally, may feel you're more calm than most, but I believe the majority of today's best and brightest judge their future every day by looking at their grade point average. It's a harsh mirror, and is, at the least, misleading. Grades are important, but they're not a measure of your future success or happiness.

# Why Grades in High School Are Important

*At college age, you can tell who's the best at taking tests and going to school, but you can't tell who the best people are. That worries the hell out of me.*

**Barnaby C. Keeney, President, Brown Univ., recalled on his death**

Before I can minimize (to an extent) the importance of grades, I have to acknowledge why they really are important. The traditional reasons are clear. It takes good grades to get into the best colleges. It takes good grades in college to get into good graduate schools, or to impress employers and get a good job. Good, that's out of the way. Realistically, if you're still aiming for the number one rated college in the country (whatever that is) and still expect to find one of those $40,000 first jobs (wherever they are), you may be right to worry about grades. If it makes you happy to spend eight years of your young life fighting for every point on every test so you can be "Number 1," I honestly wish you success. Somebody needs to do that job, and they'll need to do it well.

If your goal is to get into a college that will have a recognizable name and to have a good chance of "showing well" when interviewing for a job, yes, you better have at least a reasonable "B" average. From what I hear, there's a tremendous difference in effort, and in stress level, between Number 1 and the top 10 to 25 percent. If it takes great effort for you to get into the top 10 percent, and you can do it without ruining your health, it's worth the effort. If it takes great effort to get into the top 25 percent, and you can do it without ruining your health, it's worth the effort. Each step up in quality of results, in this case measured by grades, will make a difference, so every grade is important. I can't deny that.

There's also another higher measure of a grade's importance, at least in the way I look at them. Grades are a measurement, (although certainly sometimes a questionable measurement) of your own accomplishment. The significance I place on them is the measurement they convey to you of whether you did your best. If you know you're capable of an "A" and you got a "C," it's a measure that you didn't put out the effort you should have. If you're capable of an "A" and you got a "B," maybe you did and maybe you didn't put out enough effort. As you're quite aware by now, grades aren't always accurate measures, and often seem to be unfair.

To me, the importance of the grade is the continual motivation to reassess your own effort. If your grades aren't what you'd like them to be, then you have some thinking to do. Grades make you do that, and I think self-assessment is always important.

# Why Grades May Not Be as Important as You Think

Yes, grades are important. No, a "B" is not the end of the world. It's hard to read a newspaper or magazine these days without finding an article on grade inflation. Even *Doonesbury* spent a week on the topic. The supposed "need" by students for the highest possible grades has led supportive, although probably unwise, faculties to raise or curve grades to the point where in Honors (best and brightest) classes, it's sometimes unusual for anyone to get less than a "B." In some schools, a grade point average of 3.6 to 3.8 is no longer high enough to guarantee inclusion in the top 10 percent of the graduating class.

Most amazing of all, many schools are no longer even publishing class ranking. When the difference between 1st in the class and 50th is virtually meaningless in terms of grade point average, then the grades no longer mean anything, at least as far as colleges can use them for decision-making. Just as ridiculous are the variations in grade policies among different schools. Any college registrar who thinks a 3.9 at one school is truly comparable to a 3.9 from another school is probably quite foolish.

*The test and the use of man's education is that he finds pleasure in the exercise of his mind.*

**Jacques Berzun, Dean of the Graduate School, Columbia Univ. "Science vs. the Humanities," *Saturday Evening Post***

The result is that colleges must look to other measurements of a student's accomplishments. Standardized test scores are the most likely alternative, but even they are criticized as inappropriate for use as a decision tool when granting access to higher education.

Once grades become almost useless by themselves for measuring a student's fitness for college, the effect of each individual "A" becomes smaller. It will always be important to present as good a grade point average as you can, but the days of a college giving automatic entry to anyone with a 3.9 or better are probably over, as are the days when it took a 3.9 to get into a good school.

The best confirmation I can give you that grades are no longer the single greatest criteria for getting into a good school is a summary of statistics covering the percentage of incoming college freshmen whose grades are in the top 10 percent or the top 25 percent of their high school class. The *U.S. News and World Report 1998 College Guide* lists those statistics for 1,315 accredited colleges and universities. Based on evaluations by 4,200 college presidents, deans, and admissions directors, the schools are ranked by academic reputation (among other criteria).

What would you think the freshmen classes at the very top universities in the country look like. Do you think virtually all of the freshmen were in the top 10 percent of their high school class? Let's take a walk through the statistics and learn some surprising facts.

The table on the following pages uses the *U.S. News and World Report* data, along with information from *Peterson's Guide to Four-Year Colleges* to show some very interesting statistics about colleges and universities around the country. It highlights their acceptance rates (percentage of freshman applicants accepted) and the percentage of students in their freshman class who were in the top grade ranges of their high school class.

*I am not impressed with the Ivy League establishments. Of course they graduate the best - it's all they'll take, leaving to others the problem of educating the country. They will give you an education the way banks give you money - provided you can prove to their satisfaction that you don't need it.*

**Peter De Vries, *The Vale of Laughter***

For perspective, look first at the percentages for the services academies (West Point, Annapolis, Air Force, and the Coast Guard Academy). On average, 87 percent of their freshmen were in the top 25 percent of their high school classes, and these academies only accepted 15 percent of all applicants. There's no question that it's a challenge to get into one of the service academies. If that's your goal, it will be tough, but success will be worth the effort.

Look next at the statistics for the group identified as the "Top 26 National Universities." This list includes schools such as Harvard, Yale, Stanford, and Duke. Of their freshmen, 82 percent were in the top 10 percent of their high school class, and the schools only accepted 33 percent of their applicants. Again, those schools are pretty exclusive. Getting into them is a real accomplishment.

The interesting statistics come just after the numbers for those 30 of the 1,315 accredited colleges and universities listed. For the next 24 top national universities, including highly regarded schools like Wake Forest University, the College of William and Mary, and the University of Southern California, the top ten percentage is down to 65 percent and the acceptance rate is up to 61 percent. Even for the top 26 nationally recognized liberal arts colleges, such as Amherst College, Swarthmore, Davidson, and Vassar, the top ten percentage was only 65 percent, with an acceptance rate of 41 percent.

The remainder of the statistics become amazingly reassuring. For the national universities in the bottom half of the top 100, still including such respected schools as Boston University, Florida State, Michigan State, Purdue, and the University of Arizona, the top ten percentage was 34 percent with an acceptance rate of 74 percent! For the next tier of the top

*The average man finds life very uninteresting as it is. And I think that the reason why... is that he is always waiting for something to happen to him instead of setting to work to make things happen. For one person who dreams of making fifty thousand pounds, a hundred people dream of being left fifty thousand pounds.*

**A. A. Milne, *If I May,* "The Future"**

national liberal arts colleges, including Kenyon College, Bucknell, and Macalester, top ten was only 41 percent with an acceptance rate of 74 percent.

Moving into the category of what are called "Regional" universities and liberal arts colleges improves the percentages further without reducing the quality of the education. Schools in these categories differ from the "National" schools principally by level of funding, research, degrees and PhDs offered, and selectivity. The regional universities include high-quality schools such as Villanova, DePaul, and Santa Clara University. For schools in those categories, approximately 65 percent of their freshmen come from the top 25 percent of their high school classes and their acceptance rate is around 70 percent. For similar regional liberal arts colleges, top 25 percent totals are also around 60 percent with acceptance rates around 78 percent.

Do you understand what those statistics really say? Once you look beyond the most restrictively selective schools in the country, less than two-thirds of college freshmen come from the top 25 percent of their high school classes. That means that one third of these schools' freshmen weren't in the top 25 percent. Acceptance rates range around 70 to 80 percent. If you assume that most of the applicants not accepted probably weren't in the top 25 percent of their high school class, then the acceptance rate for those who were in the top 25 percent had to have been much higher.

On statistics alone, it should be easy to conclude that if you're in the top 25 percent of your high school class (and that's who this book is written for), there are hundreds of respected schools out there where 30 to 40 percent of the freshmen accepted will have even lower grades than you do. Furthermore, your chance of getting accepted at most of those schools is probably higher than 75 percent. How in the world can you be scared of not getting into a good college?

OK, let's try to stay realistic and take a calm look at what the numbers have shown. If you have your heart set on one of the most highly respected schools in the country, it will help to be in the top 10 percent of your high school class, and even then, the average chance of acceptance at any specific one of those schools may be less than 50 percent. If, however, you come to realize that you'll be satisfied with a degree from a recognized school where you'll get a good education and a degree that will be respected by potential employers, a position in the top 25 percent of your high school class (and solutions to the tuition challenge, which is another question), should pave your way to acceptance by such a school.

# Statistics on College Freshmen Classes

| Category - School | % of Freshmen in top 10% of HS Class | % of Freshmen in top 25% of HS Class | % Acceptance Rate |
|---|---|---|---|
| **Service Academies** | | | |
| U.S. Air Force Academy | 73 | 91 | 18 |
| U.S. Coast Guard Academy | 66 | 85 | 11 |
| U.S. Military Academy | 60 | 86 | 15 |
| U.S. Naval Academy | 61 | 85 | 15 |
| **Top 26 National Universities** (examples) | | | |
| Yale University | 95 | 99 | 18 |
| Harvard University | 90 | 100 | 11 |
| Stanford University | 87 | 97 | 16 |
| Duke University | 85 | 97 | 31 |
| Princeton University | 92 | 100 | 12 |
| Average - Top 26 | 82 | - | 33 |
| **2nd 24 National Universities** (examples) | | | |
| College of William and Mary | 74 | 94 | 48 |
| University of Southern California | 43 | 71 | 72 |
| Syracuse University | 33 | 77 | 65 |
| University of Wisconsin at Madison | 43 | 83 | 78 |
| Wake Forest University | 69 | 99 | 42 |
| Average | 65 | - | 61 |
| **Top 26 National Liberal Arts Colleges** (examples) | | | |
| Amherst College | 84 | 100 | 20 |
| Swarthmore College | 82 | 97 | 30 |
| Middlebury College | 66 | 83 | 29 |
| Oberlin College | 44 | 87 | 58 |
| Davidson College | 76 | 98 | 38 |
| Average | 65 | - | 41 |

## from U. S. News & World Report's 1998 College Guide - America's Best Colleges and Peterson's Guide to Four-Year Colleges

| Category - School | % of Freshmen in top 10% of HS Class | % of Freshmen in top 25% of HS Class | % Acceptance Rate |
|---|---|---|---|
| **Other Highly Regarded National Universities** (examples) | | | |
| Ohio State University | 23 | 47 | 85 |
| Fordham University | 26 | 61 | 70 |
| University of Arizona | 32 | 57 | 83 |
| Marquette University | 33 | 70 | 89 |
| Purdue University at West Lafayette | 25 | 60 | 90 |
| Average (2nd quartile of 228) | 34 | - | 74 |
| **Other Highly Regarded National Liberal Arts Colleges** (examples) | | | |
| Connecticut College | 46 | 66 | 43 |
| Bucknell University | 53 | 84 | 49 |
| Kenyon College (OH) | 52 | 72 | 67 |
| Macalester College | 57 | 90 | 55 |
| Average (remaining top half of 159) | 41 | - | 74 |
| **Top Regional Universities** (examples) | | | |
| Villanova University | 32 | 63 | 65 |
| Providence College | 21 | 69 | 71 |
| University of Richmond | 44 | 74 | 50 |
| Xavier University | 26 | 54 | 95 |
| Santa Clara University | 39 | 69 | 74 |
| **Top Regional Liberal Arts Colleges** (examples) | | | |
| Stonehill College (MA) | 23 | 73 | 54 |
| Mary Baldwin College (VA) | 20 | 56 | 81 |
| Carson-Newman College | 15 | 57 | 88 |
| Texas Lutheran University | 24 | 62 | 81 |

*Robert E. Lee didn't make it the first time and Jefferson Davis took the vacancy. Pershing didn't make it for two years. MacArthur couldn't get in the first year and Eisenhower took an extra year of high school to get in. [Patton] took three years to get in and five to get out.*

**Manley E. Rogers, Director of Admissions, West Point, on prominent alumni who were not initially accepted by West Point,** ***NY Times***

After all you've been warned about how hard it is to get into a good school, how can I tell you it's not as bad as you've heard? The biggest reason is that universities are competing more than ever for students. Demographic trends show fewer students available to fill colleges' future freshmen classes. Economic pressures on colleges from factors like reduced governmental funding, economic pressures, and possible overexpansion during the past good times, have created a need to recruit large freshmen classes to maintain minimum cash flow. Every factor seems to point toward easier future access to the college of your choice.

For a student safely established in the top 25 percent (or even better, the top 10 percent) of his or her high school class (my definition of today's best and brightest), acceptance into a good school should not be much of a problem. On that basis, while every grade is important, especially as it represents, to some extent, whether you're learning the things that will be important someday, each individual grade will not change your future in the way you may have been led to believe.

If you've been motivated to do well in school by fear, generated either by your parents' warnings, or by your own internal uncertainties, my wish is that you'll finally begin to take a larger view of who you are and how to measure your current preparation for life. In terms of grades, they're important. Do as well as you can. But, if you suffer when you get a "B" instead of an "A," I think you're wasting a lot of emotional energy. Put that energy into other efforts. They'll do you just as much good, and in my opinion, provide more extensive benefits over the remainder of your life.

*Universities should be safe havens where ruthless examination of realities will not be distorted by the aim to please or inhibited by the risk of displeasure.*

**Kingman Brewster, President, Yale Univ., Inaugural Address**

# What Makes the Difference in the College Admissions Process?

If you now believe that your grades are not the only, or even the most, important criteria in college admissions, then what is? Is it the SAT/ACT scores? How about those important college application essays? Maybe it's the extensive list of extracurricular activities, or the letters of reference, or the fact that you have relatives who attended the college where you want to go, or etc., etc., etc. "Tell me," I hear you say. "What's most important?"

I bet you already know what I'm going to say. If you've read this far, you know my opinion by now. Here's a hint. What do college admissions officers say they look for? They look for all of the things listed above. Some have preferences; all weight the items on the list differently. So what are they, and what am I, saying to you?

"Be the most widely talented, the most life-experienced, the most interesting person you can be."

There it is in one sentence. You don't have to be best in every category. You don't even have to be the best in any category. What you have to be is the best that you can be, in your own way, in as many ways as possible. That's an answer you've heard before, isn't it?

Well, congratulations! By reading this far, you've learned about the many ways to make yourself a more valuable person to an employer and a more attractive college applicant to an admissions officer. Those are important lessons which will serve you well. And now, for all that perseverance, you've earned the treat I promised you. A glance into the future . . . the virtual reality trip across time. I hope you enjoyed reading about the preparation, because this is where the real work begins!

*You can't start worrying about what's going to happen. You get spastic enough worrying about what's happening now.*

**Lauren Bacall**

# Chapter 9

## The "After School" Experience

Will the day ever come? Will you actually someday be finished with school, on your own, responsible entirely for yourself? Yes, one way or another, that day will someday arrive. Ready or not, school will be finished, and you'll finally meet the official definition of "adult." Will you be ready? And will the arrival produce all the rewards you've expected?

*We are so made that we can derive intense enjoyment from a contrast and very little from a state of things.*

**Sigmund Freud, *Civilization and Its Discontents***

For many people, the final arrival does feel as wonderful as promised. There can be no question that the freedoms enjoyed by adults are wonderful. Just knowing you'll never have to face another exam is reason enough to smile for several months. It's worth all the effort you expend during 16 or more years of school. So hang in there.

This third section of the book is intended to help you anticipate some of what you'll face in your first years after school. I don't think it matters that you're still in high school and that the time seems far away. If you're spending as much time fantasizing about the future as I think you are, why not insert a little realism into the fantasies? Fantasizing about the future is wonderful, especially if it helps you to plan.

In spite of the excitement your new life will hold, it's also true that a large number of new college graduates find problems adjusting to their new circumstances. Any change is stressful. The change from a structured college environment to an unstructured, independent adult environment presents enough changes to test anyone's stress management skills to the limit.

Like all the other challenges and decisions we've talked about so far, none have any reason to be feared if you've thought about them ahead of time. A little anticipation now will prevent a lot of frustration later. To be honest, simply acknowledging the likely difficulties before they arise may be sufficient to defuse the majority of them.

*God grant me the serenity to accept the things I cannot change, courage to change the things I can, and wisdom to know the difference.*

**Reinhold Niebuhr, quoted in W. Neil,** ***Concise Dictionary of Religious Quotations***

# Freedom

Admit it, it's what you've always wanted. Nobody can tell you what to do ever again. No more class schedules, no more moral obligations to parents paying the bills, nobody to account to but yourself. It sounds like heaven. Take my word, it's not.

Unless you're luckier, and much more mature, than most new graduates, you're probably quite unprepared for the changes in lifestyle you'll face during your first year out of school. Don't feel bad, everyone else before you has faced the same situation. What most haven't done is think logically and creatively about the situation ahead of time. With a little foresight, it doesn't have to be so difficult.

As human beings, we seem to search quite resolutely for predictability. We like to know what will happen each morning. But, even though we think we like to manage our own life, most of us are quite willing to let someone else make our decisions for us. If that sounds strange, remember how much of the day-to-day details of life you leave for your parents to manage. Whenever you want to make a particular decision for yourself, you'll fight to the death for the privilege, but otherwise, no big deal.

Even in school, you're quite happy to accept the schedule imposed by the environment. Sure, you think about skipping class once in a while to show your independence, but your class schedule is a comforting guarantee that someone else will take care of you. It's true, as long as you show up for class often enough, the teachers will tell you what you need to know and will make sure you know what's going to be on the tests.

If you don't believe your class schedule is designed to make life easy for you, how would you like to be without that schedule? Think about an environment where at the beginning of the semester, you're given the textbook and a list of twenty other resources. There are no classes or lectures. At unpredictable intervals, your teacher will call you to come in to take a one-on-one oral exam on any of the material from the entire course work.

Are you scared yet? I would be. While the example is rather ridiculous, it's a lot closer to a description of life after school than you might like to believe. Freedom for you means freedom for everyone else, too, and some of those "everyone elses" will still have a profound influence on your life.

My point is that for your entire life, people and society have taken care of you. In some cases, certainly, you may not have been taken care of very well, but without a doubt, that has always been the underlying goal. As long as you weren't yet an "adult," capable of taking care of yourself, somebody had to "help" you. However, someday, in the space of twenty-four hours, you will graduate, become that adult, and then, congratulations, you're on your own. Good luck in the cold, cruel world.

OK, I know I exaggerate, but it's always to make a point. Freedom means not only the right to do what you want, but the responsibility to do what you want. What do you want to do? Without anyone to make suggestions, the answer may not be easy.

*The secret of being miserable is to have leisure to bother about whether you are happy or not.*

**George Bernard Shaw, *Misalliance***

One of the first disappointments of adulthood probably is the realization that there's little positive feedback for living each day as it comes. You used to get credit for taking out the trash or making your bed, now nobody cares whether you do or not. Somebody used to smile at how you dressed when you went to class. You made such a statement either by how much or by how little effort you put into your wardrobe. Now, either no one cares, or someone is again setting a dress code. (You probably haven't had to deal with one of those since you were six years old.)

Even more staggering, you don't get grades anymore. For so many years, every few months, at least somebody told you how you were doing, and you were usually doing pretty well. Now, nobody even seems to know you're alive, let alone wants to provide any encouragement. I bet you never imagined you'd miss getting grades. That's another big surprise of adulthood.

What else has your new freedom earned you? If you're lucky enough to have found a job, it's earned you the right to get up early every weekday morning, instead of only the ones when you hadn't been able to schedule your college classes for the afternoon. What else? How about the right to work all year? No weeks off around Christmas, no spring break, and (gasp!) no summer vacation. Did you know that you've developed an internal biological clock that turns your brain off at those times? You'll just love recalibrating that clock once you're out of school.

How about the freedom to do the same thing for eight hours every day? The one hour in class, one hour relaxing, another hour of class, and an afternoon nap college schedule is history. (You know, after twenty-five years, I still miss the naps.) Anyway, the new life will hold its own set of challenges. Freedom is not all ... free.

# Friends and Family

Where did they all go? Yesterday, you had more friends than you could count. Today, they're spread out all around the country. They all have the same freedom you now have, the freedom to go out on their own. If you're back where you grew up and you're lucky, you've maintained friendships with people still in the neighborhood. If you're living in a new area, maybe one or two college friends are also in that area. Even in those situations, you (and they) are living new lives with new schedules. Your socializing will change in ways impossible to predict.

*We must rediscover the distinction between hope and expectation.*

**Ivan D. Illich, *Deschooling Society***

You may find that for the first time in your life, you actually feel alone. You may come home every night to an empty apartment with all the "freedom" of finding some way to pass the hours until bedtime. If your potential solutions to the boredom are limited by financial considerations, are you going to find yourself choosing the television as a partner? I don't care how much you enjoy TV, it's a dangerous solution.

Unless you're back living with your parents again, which presents its own considerable frustrations, your family is likely to be of less support than you might expect. For four years, you didn't need them. College life was so busy, and so much fun, it was probably a hassle to keep in touch with parents, brothers, or sisters. Now, they've developed lives attuned to their own rhythms. Sure, they still would like to hear from you, "just don't call too often (long distance charges, you know), and no, you can't fly home next week (unless you've got the money for airfare), you were here just two weeks ago. Yes, we still love you. Gotta run, though. Bye."

OK, time out. This is getting depressing, isn't it? Before you get too upset, or even worse, throw this book away, let me reassure you. I'll get to the good parts soon, I promise. This is what's known as the dose of reality to get your attention. If I don't at least raise your level of concern about life after school, you won't listen to what comes next (the good part). So, bear with me and be patient. I'm not lying about the challenges ahead, and I'm not really exaggerating either, but the good can outweigh the bad. Actually, that's what I'm here to help you realize.

## Money

If you've never been totally reliant on yourself for finances, you're in for a real challenge. Financial Truth Number One: Now and for the rest of your life, you'll never have enough money for the things you think you need to have. It seems to me you have three choices. You can continue to solicit funds from your parents, which if successful at all, will obligate you in ways not at all pleasant. You can prepare yourself for living on the streets. Or, you can learn to be financially responsible. My guess is you'll find all three almost equally unattractive.

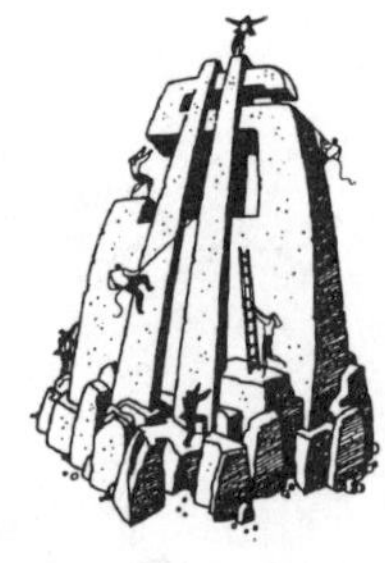

At the very least, you'll get to manage a checking account, take care of a car, furnish a place to live, and limit your spending on entertainment to leave some money for food. Oh yes, you'll get to pay taxes, too. Let's not forget how much fun tax returns can be. Unless you're a financial obsessive/compulsive (like the author of this book), you're going to find personal finance is just one more example of how the world is out to get you.

## On the Job

I've already talked about what your first post-college job will probably involve. If you remember, I wasn't too encouraging about that aspect of life, either. To remind you (sorry), first jobs are not usually exciting, rewarding experiences. They're testing grounds, chances to prove yourself. And they're often the work that nobody else wants to do. Let's not spend any more time on this subject. The boss is probably watching.

*Youth would be an ideal state if it came a little later in life.*

**Earl Asquith, quoted in *Quote and Unquote***

## Summary

Finishing college is not the end of your life's challenges; it's really only the beginning. Fortunately, there are ways to face those challenges that can make the effort exciting and rewarding. Those include understanding what lies ahead and preparing yourself to handle whatever comes. The rest of this book is about just that. I like to think of it as "the good part," not just of the book, but of life itself.

*To understand the nature of happiness we first have to know what it means to eat one's fill.. It's not a matter of how much you eat, but of the way you eat. It's the same with happiness - it doesn't depend on the actual number of blessings we manage to scratch from life, but only our attitude towards them.*

**Alexander Solzhenitsyn, *The First Circle***

# Chapter 10

## A Fulcrum, A Lever, and a Place to Stand

*I've always felt that a person's intelligence is directly reflected by the number of conflicting points of view that he can entertain simultaneously on the same topic.*

**Lisa Alther, *Kinflicks***

If the last chapter presented the challenge, this one is meant to offer a solution. Not "the" solution, because you have to find that for yourself, but an approach, a way to face the future with hope and a bit of confidence. That's really what you need the most, the self-confidence to believe in yourself and the knowledge that you can be as well-prepared for life as anyone. Once you know you're the best resource around, the future will look much brighter, even on the cloudy days.

You physicists understand the title of this chapter, don't you? The claim by Archimedes is one of the best known maxims of the physical sciences and is taught to all high school physics students. "Give me a fulcrum, a lever, and a place to stand, and I'll move the world." One of the beauties of the statement is its simplicity. With only a little thought, even the non-scientist can understand the principle. With the proper tools, the correct angle, and a sturdy base of support, there is nothing that can't be moved.

My exciting promise to you is that you can apply that simple physical principle to your life after college, and just as effectively, to your life right now. All you need is a "fulcrum," a "lever," and "a place to stand," and you, too, can move the world. Once you decide what each of those three resources mean to you, make sure you have them, then go out and get busy. It's actually more easy to shove the world around than you may think, at least it's possible within that little bit of the world you occupy. That's all you need to move, you know. Make a ripple in your own pond, and the waves will flow out in all directions.

Personally, I don't think you need to know my choices for each of those three important factors. I'd rather you decide for yourself what's most significant. One, however, may be the education you've already attained. Another may be the experiences you've already had. Others might include the way you believe the world ought to be, the respect you have for the earth itself, or the faith you have in a power beyond this world.

*If you cannot catch a bird of paradise, better take a wet hen.*

**Nikita S. Khrushchev, Soviet Premier, *Time***

My hope is that one of your three tools will be a conviction to become the best that you can possibly imagine. That's surely a daunting goal, but one that will pay dividends beyond your current ability to measure. It's a goal that you won't attain overnight, but day by day as you learn and grow. You'll find such an accomplishment through your own efforts. What I can do is identify certain crossroads that you're likely to reach.

What I'll offer are suggestions for aspects of your life where you may find room for enhancement. What I hope is that these after-college suggestions will be every bit as relevant to the challenges you face in high school. Like my suggestions for improving your job prospects, I want to help you find ways to improve your life prospects. Again, they're not meant to be considered all at once, but a little bit at a time. Baby steps, remember? That's all it takes.

## Physical Health

How much do you usually accomplish on days when you're ill? Every day for the rest of your life, the way you view each day, and the success you find in it, will be influenced greatly by how well you feel. Unfortunately, you can't prevent yourself from getting sick once in a while. What you can do, however, is optimize your health. One of the first important steps in building a happy life is, without a doubt, building a healthy life. The primary concerns are diet and exercise.

Your first year out of school may be the first time you've ever had to be totally responsible for your own meals. Even if that's not the case, the stresses you'll be facing will be much different from those you've dealt with so far. The extra stress will put an actual, physical strain on your body. If all the other challenges in your life lead to neglect of your physical needs, it won't take long for your body to let you know it's not happy.

Few young people enjoy cooking. We've all gotten so used to fast food, it feels like a burden to cook anything that takes longer than five minutes to prepare. If you really want to address two of the topics in this chapter at once, you might consider adopting cooking as a hobby. Not only will that contribute mightily to your health, but it can add an impressive dimension to your social life.

*Happiness is like coke - something you get as a by-product in the process of making something else.*

**Aldous Huxley, *Point Counter Point***

More likely, you'll have to find some way to integrate the need for healthy nourishment with a busy lifestyle and your lack of desire to cook. Fortunately, prepared foods these days are far more nutritional and appetizing than you might expect. If you learn what you need to know about nutrition, you're willing to plan ahead, and you read and understand product labels, you can take care of your dietary requirements with at least a bit of variety. It may not nourish your soul, but at least you won't starve.

The other food issue to remember is financial. Subsisting on fast food and prepared foods will be more expensive than buying and preparing meals yourself. If you're on a really tight budget, you may have to learn to economize. On the other hand, saving money on food takes careful planning. Cooking for one can leave leftovers that are often wasted. You can lose your cost savings quite easily through waste.

Effective dietary planning and efficient food preparation can easily be books of their own. You had better find a way to learn what you need to know. I promise you that neglecting your diet will be a first step on the road to misery. If you need extra insurance, take your vitamins (after learning what's helpful and what's not). Even if you decide against making food a rewarding, soul satisfying part of your life, please make it a first priority to give your body the fuel it needs.

After making sure that your body has the nourishment it needs, you've still got work to do. It doesn't matter in the least whether your job or your lifestyle necessitate a high level of physical activity, you had better do something to get in shape.

Admittedly, if you're relatively healthy and you eat right, you can get by reasonably well without a regular exercise program. Especially if you're young, you probably won't notice any obvious effects of lack of exercise. What you will suffer, without knowing it, is a slow but steady depletion of your energy reserves.

I'm far from an expert in physical conditioning, but I do know that the less you exercise, the less you feel like exercising. Conversely, the more you exercise (within reason), the better you feel. If you're not convinced, do some reading on the effects of exercise. You'll find that people who exercise regularly get sick less often, are able to withstand more physical exertion, and at least believe they're better able to deal with emotional stress than people who don't exercise.

That last fact is more important than you may realize. If as a result of something you do, you think you feel better, then you do feel better. It doesn't matter to me whether the effect of a regular exercise program truly is better physical health or only a personal impression that you feel better, the results will be the same.

*Suffering isn't ennobling, recovery is.*
**Christiaan N. Barnard,** ***NY Times***

The goal you're considering in this section of this book is finding ways to feel better about yourself and your life. I propose to you that a regular exercise program will actually improve your overall health and will enable you to manage effectively more of the stresses you're going to face every day. At the least, I believe such a program will make you think you can accomplish more. That works for me.

An effective exercise program doesn't have to involve an expensive health club or high-tech exercise equipment. Buy a second hand bike, get a $20 tennis racquet, save up for some good jogging shoes, or just walk every day. If you don't live in an area where you feel comfortable walking or riding a bike after work, save some of your entertainment budget until you can afford some piece of home exercise equipment. It's that important.

If you do decide to buy something, be sure to get something you'll use. In my opinion, an ideal piece of equipment is one that's either so much fun to use that you can't wait to get back to it (find one for me, please) or is designed so you can do something else while you exercise. My favorites of the latter variety are exercise bikes or stair machines. I've found that I can read while I'm using either one. That's another "two-fer," accomplishing two personal enhancement activities at once.

Rowing machines, weight-training systems, or even jump ropes still allow you to watch television while you exercise. I don't usually recommend television, but if it gets you to exercise regularly, why not? Every week when you watch *Home Improvement*, do some Body Improvement at the same time. Even better (forgive me, Tim Allen), if I haven't convinced you yet that reading for entertainment is wonderful, start renting movies that may help to expand your understanding of the world.

The same result can be obtained with *Books on Tape*, cable channels like *The Discovery Channel*, or *The Learning Channel*, and don't forget the wonderful programs on traditional Public TV stations. Your opportunities for improving your body and your mind at the same time are many. I really can't encourage you strongly enough to invest the time necessary to make your body all it can be. It will set the tone for the accomplishing the same thing with your mind, and with your life.

## Environment

One of the biggest excitements for me about becoming an adult was establishing my first home. I believe that even more than your first car, the first apartment or residence you can call your own establishes your freedom, independence, and adulthood. Even twenty-five years later, I can remember as clearly as if it were yesterday the feeling of that first moment after the furniture and the boxes were all inside, the friends who'd helped me move had left, and I was absolutely alone in my home. I sat there and did nothing but stare at the blank walls for at least fifteen minutes. It was one of the most satisfied feelings I've ever had.

It doesn't matter what kind of a dump it may be, if it's yours and it's home, that's all that matters. I encourage you to look forward with the greatest anticipation to your first place. Unless your parents are wiser than most, they'll probably express concern about how small or dirty it seems, or how dangerous the neighborhood is. Their opinions do have some relevance, so don't completely ignore them, but don't let them rain on your parade, either. It's a new world you're creating, not a reflection of theirs. It's your job, on your own small scale (as well as on a much larger one), to take what you're given and make it better than anyone else has yet imagined.

*Man must choose to be rich in things or in the freedom to use them.*

**Ivan D. Illich, *Deschooling Society***

When the time does come to establish your first home, it's critical that you do make it truly your own. Whether you're sharing it with someone else, or not, whether it's next door to your parents, or on the other side of the country, celebrate the event as a true beginning of your life. There are few life events that will carry more significance.

As your home will reflect you and how you view the world, you should put some significant effort into making it a bright, happy, encouraging place to be. What that means in terms of specifics only you can decide. The goal is to make your home a place where you feel comfortable, both physically and psychologically. On the assumption that you'll have stressful, low points in your life once in a while, make your home a place that will help you recover a positive viewpoint whenever that effort becomes necessary.

Your new home is much more than the place you sleep every night, it's made up of layers that extend outward as far as you're willing to admit. Think about it. The first layer, of course, is inside those walls where you live. The second layer is your next door neighbors or maybe a roommate. Next is your immediate neighborhood and all the many people, social systems, and life experiences waiting to be explored. Outside that layer is your larger town or city, your state, your country, and the entire world we inhabit.

You realize, I hope, that these layers are not specifically geographic. You have similar layers of relationships with people. There are the closest relationships such as roommates, your primary romantic interest, and (I hope), your family. Outer layers can include best friends, people you relate to every day, people you know as acquaintances, and even people you don't know personally, but who are part of your world nonetheless. Don't ever imagine that politicians, representatives of businesses you use, and even celebrities who entertain you are not a real part of your world and your life. They influence you, and through your support (or lack of it), you influence theirs.

*One is happy as a result of one's own efforts, once one knows those necessary ingredients of happiness - simple tastes, a certain degree of courage, self denial to a point, love of work, and, above all, a clear conscience. Happiness is no vague dream, of that I now feel certain.*

**George Sand, *Correspondence*, *Vol. V***

Everything you do affects many, if not all of those outward layers. And everything that happens in those layers affects you, no matter how tightly you wrap yourself in your four little walls. When you reach the stage in your life that you begin to create your "home" for the future, use that opportunity to consider the entire environment you're going to be inhabiting.

There are millions of aspects of that environment you can't change overnight to suit your own wishes, but there are none that can't be changed over time as you build your world of the future. Use that mind set to build a first outer layer that is representative of what you hope for in all the other layers you're going to inhabit.

## Possessions

How much "stuff" do you have? How much does it mean to you? Whether possessions should, or shouldn't, be so important is an interesting question. My answer to that one, like my answer to most other questions is, it depends. Do you pass judgment on your, or other people's, success by how much stuff they have? Is it your goal to accumulate as much money as you can, so you can have as many nice things as possible? If so, are you a bad person? Again, it depends.

Let me explain. If you are so shallow that your life is driven solely by a competitive urge to have more "things" than anyone else, if your happiness is based solely on checking off items on a laundry list of desired acquisitions, I'd say you're probably going to end up unhappy.

The most likely reason for that result is the impossibility that you're going to be successful enough to win that race. There will always be many, many people who have more than you do. What's most likely is it will usually seem everyone has more than you do. I guarantee that will be a misperception, but it will feel that way. If your evaluation of personal success rests on that type of comparison, you're going to conclude someday that the world is unfair, or that you are a loser. The first conclusion is probably correct. The second is ridiculous. Neither helps you at all.

So many people scream at you about avoiding dependence on "things" that it's easy to conclude you should never let "things" come to mean anything significant to you. I disagree. There are many reasons to value your possessions. I'd rather you come to understand a reasonable way to enjoy the happiness your possessions can bring.

One of my earliest happy memories is the first game I bought with my own allowance. I saved my money, walked to the store alone, bought the game, and spent untold hours playing with it. I was proud of it because, in my opinion, I had earned the right to have it. The same feeling attached to my first car that I bought. I worked all summer, seven days a week from 4:30 a.m. until 1:00 p.m. (honest) to pay for a five-year old car. I loved that car; I even gave it a name.

*You can have anything you want if you want it desperately enough. You must want it with an exuberance that erupts through the skin and joins the energy that created the world.*

**Sheilah Graham,**
***The Rest of the Story***

The point of those two love affairs with things is what they actually represented. Neither "thing" had any great material value. I doubt anyone else would even have wanted them. To me, however, they were priceless. They represented the result of personal effort; seeing them made me proud. They made me feel good about myself. What greater meaning could a possession have?

Do you have certain things that are very dear to you? Do they mean more to you than just their dollar value? If you understand the difference between taking great personal pleasure from a possession and using things to try to establish your value to other people, you have the potential to find a lot of happiness in your life. I've always found that I, and most people, can find a way to have any one material thing I want, I just can't have every material thing I want. Coming to a satisfactory acceptance of that fact makes it possible to choose a special possession and to take incredible pleasure out of the acquisition and care of that item.

There will be few enough opportunities for true happiness in life, so finding a "thing" that will bring you happiness, working to obtain it, and enjoying the possession of it, even if it's something you can only look at, like a painting, can bring a great deal of satisfaction to your life. A thing, by itself, can never be enough to fill your entire requirement for happiness, but you certainly have my permission to choose one or two to treat with affection. Like a trustworthy friend, they can be there for you when you need them.

*It is not the level of prosperity that makes for happiness but the kinship of the heart and the way we look at the world. Both attitudes are within our power, so that a man is happy so long as he chooses to be happy, and no one can stop him.*

**Alexander Solzhenitsyn, *Cancer Ward***

# Emotional Health

There are many areas that influence you on an emotional level. No matter how well you arrange your physical environment, it will always be what goes on in your head that controls whether you're going to be happy or not. I believe, and what I write is based on the assumption, that it is possible to be happy with very little in the way of material possessions. Even poor health or disabilities don't have to prevent a person from being happy.

As you embark on adulthood, you have a golden opportunity to consider what's going to be important to you during the rest of your life. It shouldn't be a surprise that every time you pass a milestone in your life, you'll almost automatically reevaluate what aspects of your existence have importance and meaning to you. Finishing school, both high school and college, are certainly two of those times.

Now, when you truly are establishing patterns that will affect the remainder of your years, you face one of the best chances you'll ever have to design your life for happiness. My desire for you is that at this very important point in your life you take an honest, wide-eyed look around you and see what looks good about the world.

Don't be discouraged if you're not too happy with what you see. Few of us ever "have it all together." What you do have is time, and nearly unlimited opportunity. What exists today will be different tomorrow. Now is the time to decide what you'd like tomorrow to look like. Once you do, you can then begin to turn it into what you'd like it to be. To help you think of places to start, these next sections will simply remind you of areas in your life that are waiting for your attention.

## Friends/Family/Significant Others

There's no avoiding the fact that the people you spend your life with will have an immense influence on your efforts to be happy. If you currently have one or more special people in your life who do make you very happy, you're lucky. Because people continually change, and because it is so easy to lose someone you care for, take advantage of your current happiness. Let your special people know how much they mean to you. Celebrate their presence in your life whenever possible.

If I had to give you one special piece of advice about how to maintain what is already a positive relationship, I'd suggest that you expect the relationship, and both people in the relationship, to change continually. No matter how wonderful a relationship may be, to stay alive, it has to grow. Any other expectation will lead to disappointment. If you can accept this truth, you should try to make any successful relationship you have a joint exploration of the world you share. Give your partner frequent chances to explore on his or her own, and always be enthusiastic and interested in sharing what either of you has discovered.

That concept applies equally well to friends, family, and any romantic interests you may find. Give everyone you care for room to experience life as they understand it. Take an active interest in what motivates them, whether it's important to you, or not. If they are important to you, their concerns become a part the environment in which you live. Remember the layers?

*Every person, all the events in your life are there because you have drawn them there. What you choose to do with them is up to you.*

**Richard Bach,**
***Illusions: Adventures of a Reluctant Messiah***

Take the time to share with them the things that are important to you. True, they may not always appear interested. You don't need to push yourself and your ideas on anyone. But try not to give someone the opportunity to come to you someday and tell you that they, "don't know who you are anymore." If you're going to change as you grow and mature, give the people you care for the chance to grow and change with you. Then, it's up to them to join you on your journey, or choose a different road. That's their right, as it is yours, also.

A happy, open, warm, and sharing person who allows others to have the freedom to become whatever they want to be is the most attractive individual on the face of the earth. Not only will becoming such a person create the best opportunity to keep wonderful people a part of your life, it will attract an ever larger group of similar people into your circle of friends. Become the person who you want to have care for you. It's a no-lose proposition.

What do you do, however, if there are people in your life who make you feel miserable? If you care enough about them to want them in your life, you have to acknowledge that you're going to continue to feel miserable until you find some way to change the relationship as it currently exists.

*What interests me isn't the happiness of every man, but that of each man.*

**Boris Vian,**
***L'Ècume des Jours***

Can I tell you how to build (or rebuild) your relationships with the important people in your life? With most of them, there's too much history between you and them to expect you can make major changes, especially if you're expecting the other person to do the changing. If your hope is that with a little effort, you can make your mother/father/best friend/ girlfriend/ boyfriend into the person you want them to be, you've already got a problem bigger than I can address.

Another great rule for life is, "There's very little you can do to change anyone you know into someone more compatible with you." In a way, it's a bit of an insult to think you have the right to try. All you can ever expect to do to change your life is to change yourself.

So what do you do if someone in your life is a source of frustration, if spending a significant portion of the rest of your life with them is likely to cause you unhappiness? In many cases, the answer is that you have to choose a different road. It's not a decision to take lightly, but you're better off by yourself than being with someone who makes you miserable. Whether it means giving up friends, a significant other, or even a spouse, the time sometimes comes when it's not only desirable, it's actually necessary.

If you're currently facing a decision about whether to strike out on your own, or if because of your new circumstances in life you find that you're already alone, I really want you to know that lonely times can be blessings, too. I don't want you to fear being alone, because it doesn't have to be a lost time, and it almost always lasts for a shorter time than you expect.

My first lonely time after college led me to get involved in volunteer work. There I literally met hundreds of wonderful people. Some became my best friends, a few I came to care for deeply. Today, my life is more full than I can imagine, in spite of a lonely time when I felt I'd never find anyone special.

What I didn't anticipate during that time was that I'd find myself before I found someone else. That was the most special "find" of all. The hope I hold out to you is that no matter how lonely it may be to be by yourself for a while, during that time, you can become an even more wonderful person than you are right now. It actually helps to be on your own when you're searching for what you really want in life. It clears your mind to evaluate choices with few outside influences. There's nobody else telling you, either directly or indirectly, what should be important to you. It's a valuable experience, no matter how painful it may seem at the time.

Your challenge is to refuse to be so afraid of being alone that you accept suffering or even basic dissatisfaction as the best you can imagine. Happiness often involves risk. If you develop the strength within yourself to know what you really want from life, then risking loneliness to find true happiness will always be worth the gamble.

What, however, if the person you can't get along with still means so very much to you that you can't imagine being without them? To me, that includes anyone who's a member of your immediate family. I believe you face two primary options. First, you need to be very sure you're the person you really think you should be.

Remember, no problem in a relationship is ever solely the fault of one person. There are few saints on this earth, and you should at least be humble enough to doubt that you're one of those few. If you truly care about someone, it shouldn't be necessary for you to require a specific improvement from them for every improvement you make in yourself. If you acknowledge there are things about yourself that might be changed for the better, then you've discovered a completely separate issue from how someone else may need to improve themselves.

*People change and forget to tell each other.*

**Lillian Hellman, *Toys in the Attic***

Are you willing to concentrate on being the best "partner" you can be, whether they are willing to make any changes or not? Are you willing to take the initiative yourself to make the relationship healthy on at least one side, even if it takes a week, a month, or a year? Until you can say "yes" to that question, and follow it up with action, you haven't done your full part to make the world a happier place.

It's still possible that after all your work to improve yourself, you may see no improvement in "them," or in the relationship, at all. What do you do, then? If you have a choice, please choose the potential for future happiness. The pain of separation will be no worse than the pain of togetherness, and the potential for true happiness somewhere in the future can carry you through many less than wonderful todays.

If you don't feel you have a choice to make a change (family relationships included), the option to stay is actually a choice, isn't it? If a person is

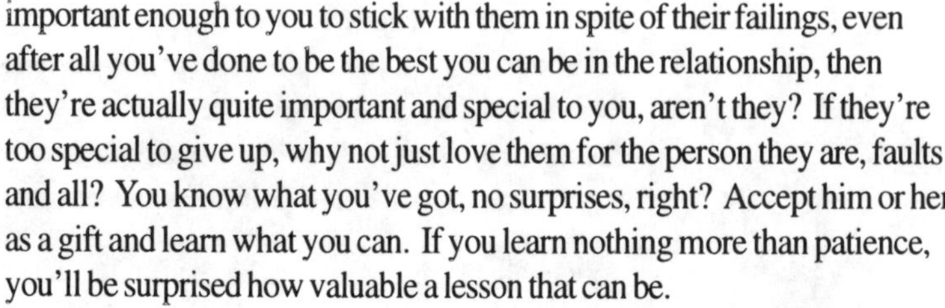

important enough to you to stick with them in spite of their failings, even after all you've done to be the best you can be in the relationship, then they're actually quite important and special to you, aren't they? If they're too special to give up, why not just love them for the person they are, faults and all? You know what you've got, no surprises, right? Accept him or her as a gift and learn what you can. If you learn nothing more than patience, you'll be surprised how valuable a lesson that can be.

*If you want something very, very badly, let it go free. If it comes back to you, it's yours forever. If it doesn't, it was never yours to begin with.*

**Jesse Lair,**
***I Ain't Much, Baby – But I'm All I've Got***

I think you're going to find that personal relationships will challenge you throughout your life more than any other opportunity you face. If you always try to live by the assumption that everyone you meet is doing the best they can based on the way they view the world and that you probably aren't doing quite as good a job as you are able, you'll at least have a chance to build healthy relationships with most people you meet. Share of yourself generously, and acknowledge with appreciation what others are willing to share with you. As you learn to appreciate and love yourself more, you will find that others are able to appreciate and love you more, also.

## Happiness and Your Job

No matter how strongly you may think that life after school is focused on your first job, I happen to believe it's only one part of defining who you are as an adult. It's important, and it does have considerable power to affect your happiness, but it's most certainly not all that matters.

Your first job is bound to be "entry level," in all aspects of what that means. The chances are really high that you're not going to feel challenged and rewarded by the responsibilities you're assigned. You are going to find yourself facing another set of tests. Unfortunately, the things you're going to be tested on are not the interesting topics you studied in school, but the qualities of patience, stamina, and concentration. Your first year or two are going to be a maturity-check. Some fun, right?

If what we're talking about here is happiness, how does such a job fit into the picture? Maybe you'll be lucky and you will find a rewarding job right away. If so, be thankful and take full advantage of the opportunity. But if your first job is typical, it may not provide an experience that sends you home happy every night. What then?

The key, I believe, is an attitude that will be valuable in all aspects of your life. Don't be afraid to have lofty desires, goals, and ambitions, but always be sure to maintain realistic expectations. That's especially important in terms of time frames. You have a right to expect a satisfying, challenging, engaging job someday, but you may have to spend a little time preparing for and finding it.

If you're mentally prepared for the longer term aspects of building a career, you'll be much better prepared for the day-to-day frustrations of your first few jobs. It's normal to come home from work some days convinced that you can't stand "that place" another minute. If it doesn't come as such a surprise and shock when you feel that way, you should be able to realize it's not the end of the world. You'll be able to turn your attention to other important concerns in your life and let the job problem work itself out over time.

*Adults are obsolete children.*

**Dr. Seuss, quoted in L. L. Levinson, *Bartlett's Unfamiliar Quotations***

That's often the most healthy approach to frustrations you'll encounter at every stage of your life. Unless a problem literally screams for immediate attention, it's often better to find a more valuable area to concentrate on foı a while. Especially in relation to the jobs you'll hold soon after college, spend your emotional energy on interests that will bring more immediate enjoyment. You don't always need to wait until next year to be happy. You just need to learn how to focus your efforts in the directions that bring the greatest rewards.

What we're talking about is building a life that will bring you happiness over many years. Sure, everyone wants to be happy each and every day of their lives. That may be our most basic human desire. Unfortunately, being happy every single minute of every day is impossible. Life is too difficult and complicated to expect such perfection.

The only reasonable goal therefore is to search for as much happiness as you can find. Understanding what that means and conducting a logical search will create the highest likelihood of success. In my opinion, finding and developing a large number of things that make you happy is the best approach.

There will be days when your job frustrates you. There will be days when the people you care for are causing you problems, or maybe there will be times when there is no special person in your life. Some days you won't feel particularly well. There will even be days when all of those challenges occur at the same time. Those are also usually the days when the television breaks. What are you going to do to convince yourself that life is still worth living?

## Hobbies

Now is the time to begin adding more than just the basics to your life's enjoyments. Finding one or more hobbies that hold real meaning for you will be more valuable than you can imagine. If at your lowest moments, you know there is always something you enjoy doing, some activity that doesn't take extensive preparation, special circumstances, or other people, you'll always have the peace of mind that comes from knowing you can focus your attention on at least one positive action.

*The whole of art is an appeal to a reality which is not without us but in our minds.*

**Desmond MacCarthy, *Modern Drama***

It's hard to imagine you've gotten to this point in your life without developing some interests beyond work, school, friends, and television. If you stop and think for five minutes, you can probably remember nearly a dozen interests you've had at different times in your life. If you don't already have a favorite hobby, think about those past interests and consider reinvestigating one of them.

There really are adult equivalents or extensions of your childhood interests. Many of the items that interested you as children (dolls, baseball cards, comic books) are now collectors' items. You may already have the basis for a valuable hobby packed away in your attic. If you used to belong to a young person's group (Boy Scouts, Girl Scouts, church groups, etc.), why not consider becoming an adult advisor? There are uncounted advantages in that idea.

Need more money? Why not consider a hobby that produces something valuable you can sell, or involves a service you can provide? If you sew or crochet, if you like to work on cars, if you like gardening, or if you're a good cook, the number of talents with commercial value are unlimited. Anything you like to do that someone else doesn't like to do can earn you money while adding enjoyment to your own life. The only limits are your own imagination.

The ideal personal situation is, in my opinion, to have so many interests that there's always something you've been anxious to get around to, but haven't had the time. A successful hobby doesn't have to be something on which you spend ten hours a week. That's why enjoying many different things is just as valuable as having one overwhelming special interest. In my case, I sometimes feel that even if I didn't have my job, I'd still have so many things to do that I wouldn't be able to find enough time. I realize that's not true, but the fact that it seems that way makes me feel my life is full and rewarding.

The whole idea is to build enough variety and rewards into your life that there's always something positive. In the overall effort to create a happy life, giving yourself the greatest number of enjoyable alternatives has to be the place to start.

## Where Do We Go from Here?—A Transition

I've come to realize while writing this book that happiness is virtually an undefinable concept. No one can reliably determine what will make another person happy. There really is no way I can present myself as an authority on what you should do to be happy. No one but you is qualified to do that.

Still, I feel a strong inner motivation to do something to help you along your path. There seems to be so much dissatisfaction and disappointment in the world today, especially among young people. While a lot of it is justified, and much hard work does need to be done to solve some difficult problems, this is still a beautiful world with incredible opportunities.

I believe achieving maturity means learning to acknowledge the difficulties and failures in the world while still being able to take great joy in the wonders of life. I believe there is a way to learn how to do that. It's nowhere near as simple as checking off items on a list of "happiness issues," but it is an approach worth considering. What I will write from this point, then, will be less a set of specific suggestions and more a way to look at life. I think you'll find it challenging, but if you've read this far, I think you're ready. I hope it will help you in your search.

*If he [a teacher] is indeed wise, he does not bid you enter the house of his wisdom, but rather leads you to the threshold of your own mind.*

**Kahlil Gibran, *The Prophet*, "Of Teaching"**

# Chapter 11

## What I Hope You're Really Seeking — Putting a Little "Soul" in Your Life

*If you want knowledge, you must take part in the changing of reality. If you want to know the taste of a pear, you must change the pear by eating it yourself.*

**Mao Tse-Tung, Quotations from Chairman Mao Tse-Tung**

To be honest, the discussion to this point about "being happy" actually may be a bit shallow for what I really want you to find. I realize you've probably spent fifteen to twenty years of your life thinking that's exactly what you've been aiming for, and you're not alone. The majority of people in all the world also think of their personal goals in terms of those very words. In my opinion, you deserve more than that. If you truly want to be happy, to have a life you'll feel is satisfying and successful, I believe you need to seek something beyond the concept of "happy."

There may not be a perfect word for the state of being I would wish for you. Personal satisfaction is so undefinable, I can't even set for you a clear target. But I do want to share with you an important concept presented in *Care of the Soul*, a recent book by Thomas Moore.

I received the book as a Christmas present. By the time I had the chance to read it, I was already deeply in the middle of writing this book. I knew I was coming to the section of the book where I was going to talk to you about happiness, and I wasn't sure how to approach the subject.

To quote one of my favorite great truths of life, "When the student is ready, the teacher appears." I think Thomas Moore showed up for me at just the right time. (An interesting thought: You're reading this book, are you now a ready student, also?)

Moore, in 17 years as a psychotherapist, probably heard every possible complaint about unsuccessful efforts to find happiness. His patients spoke of disappointment, disillusionment, fears, and failures. Their real pain was a sense of emptiness, a feeling that their lives lacked meaning. What they wanted was fulfillment, a conviction that they mattered, that the actions which made up their everyday lives were important. Moore called the missing aspect in their lives "Soul."

*It is the soul's duty to be loyal to its own desires. It must abandon itself to its master passion.*

**Rebecca West, Quoted by A. L. Rowse, *Glimpses of the Great University***

The word soul has had so many meanings to so many different people and cultures, it's probably difficult to build a definition not clouded by earlier shadings. If you feel you're influenced too greatly by past definitions, try simply to choose a new, unfamiliar word to substitute for the word soul. The goal is to approach the word with no boundaries or limitations. Don't even think of it as a noun, at least not yet. Let the concept develop as you consider what it might mean to you.

To me, Moore's definition of Soul calls for a recognition and appreciation of the wonders of life. In everything that happens to us are the seeds of Soul. I think of the words "richness" and "depth" when I try to imagine the description of a life connected with Soul. Moore uses examples of experiences which can cultivate Soul, such as, "good food, satisfying conversation, genuine friends, and experiences that stay in the memory and touch the heart."

If his words don't strike a chord, think of the best of experiences you can remember. Remember times with friends or with one very special person. Remember a beautiful day when everything was just the way you would have dreamed it. All of us are fortunate enough to have had a few of those times. When that day was done and you wished to save the feeling deep inside of you, so you'd never, ever forget it, what was that moment like? At that moment, when you felt you understood the best of what life could be, you were in touch with one of the aspects of Soul.

What's critically significant in Moore's interpretation of Soul, however, is that he includes in his list of Soulful times not just the exciting, satisfying, happy experiences of life, but also the sad, painful, distressing experiences. For every time of peace, there will be times of suffering; for times of trusting love, there will be times of jealousy; with joys of attachment, will come sadness of loss.

Does searching for Soul then mean that the unhappy times can't be avoided? Every honest view of life indicates that's the case. The realization that bad times will occur for every individual is so universal that any theory of life attempting to challenge that expectation is doomed to failure. Moore's desire in the search for Soul is an honest acceptance of the complexities of life and a recognition that in every experience is meaning, and Soul.

Maybe the "rules of life" require that we experience all types of pain. Maybe our purpose in life is simply that, to experience the best of times and the worst of times, and to learn as much as possible from both.

I guess that idea forces you to address your most basic question about life itself. Does life have any purpose? If you're comfortable with the concept that life may truly have a purpose, that humanity is not an accident, then the desire to find that purpose and live in harmony with it should have an attraction. The care of the Soul focuses on accepting the search for Soul as a search for meaning in life. Finding one implies finding the other.

But what if you don't believe in life being anything other than a biological quirk of fate? Is there any hope of finding Soul in your life? I think Moore would say yes. What you're looking for, just like everyone else, is your own definition of meaning in your life. All you really want is a way to view your current existence as worthwhile. If Moore's care of the Soul allows you to find the depth and richness that you seek, who cares whether we're here by design or by accident? It's here and now that counts, right?

So it seems we're all eligible for an approach to life that helps us feel we have purpose and meaning. If you're interested, I'll tell you more about Thomas Moore's recommendations, and about my own. I think he and I wish for you pretty much the same things. You can call it happiness if you wish, but I think it's more, much more.

*The only books that influence us are those for which we are ready and which have gone a little further down our particular path than we have yet gone ourselves.*

**E. M. Forster, recalled on his death**

## Search for the Soul

Reading Thomas Moore's book is a deep, rich, rewarding experience. In fact, I imagine he felt connected with Soul as he wrote it, and intended that we all feel Soul as we read it. It's a good example of what I would call, "being in touch with the essence of life." For me, it's that feeling that tells me I'm experiencing a Soul experience. When I sense that something happening to me has a certain intensity, when I feel that if I only knew exactly how to "see" the event properly, there would be an important message there somewhere, then I know there's Soul involved.

Another concept that may help you understand Soul, and another good word for an experience that has connections to Soul, is also the title of a wonderful book by Mihaly Csikszentmihalyi, *Flow: The Psychology of Optimal Experience*. You're probably already vaguely familiar with the concept of flow. It's used often these days in connection with sports experiences. An athlete who has gotten "into a zone" where almost nothing can go wrong often describes the experience as feeling drawn along by a flow, by an invisible current that made his or her actions come as

easily and naturally as floating down a river. Any event that can absorb your concentration to the extent you almost lose touch with "normal" reality can connect you with the feeling of flow and probably also the experience of Soul.

*Life forms illogical patterns. It is haphazard and full of beauties which I try to catch as they fly by, for who knows whether any of them will ever return?*

**Margot Fonteyn,**
***Margot Fonteyn***

While you may never have consciously experienced it before, flow can occur in many very simple experiences. The set when every tennis ball landed just inside the line, the romantic date when you said all the right things (for once), even the test where all the answers just seemed to pop into your mind. Each was an experience of flow and a positive experience of Soul.

Flow is virtually always positive, a rush of good feelings while engaged in concentrated, purposeful effort. Research shows that the experience of flow usually has a measurable physical effect on the body. Athletes say they reach states where their bodies are able to do more than is capable by pure will alone. Artists say they attain a connection with an invisible power that inspires their efforts and enables amazing creative accomplishments. Even people who say they feel flow in their regular daily activities seem to exhibit lower stress levels and live more healthy existences.

I would say experiencing flow in an activity is an indication that there is Soul involved. I don't, however, think that they're really the same thing. Thomas Moore's concept of Soul is much more complex than the idea of flow. Soul is the hunger inside of us that feeds on a conscious recognition, appreciation, and interaction with life. Flow, while it may sometimes feel like a more keen awareness of life, is actually a disconnection from the larger experience of life, a momentary intense connection with a small segment of existence. Soul may also be focused at any given moment in a specific event, but its true desire is that the event fit somehow into the wider patterns of our world.

For me, the concept of Soul exists almost entirely in the belief that events do happen for a reason. This may present a challenge to some people who question the existence of an "unseen power" influencing events in the world, so I need to address that question first. While Soul does fit comfortably into a belief that there is such an unseen power, it's not necessary to accept that belief to understand and benefit from the concept of Soul. The way I read Moore's ideas, Soul can even be seen as a part of ourselves, something existing "inside" our hearts or minds.

This dual nature of Soul makes it reasonable to visualize the search for Soul in two different ways. It's certainly logical to believe that God or some other great power does have a plan for each life. On that basis, the search for Soul involves trying to align our lives with that "great Plan." The duality of Soul makes it equally acceptable to assume that we each have an inherent knowledge inside of us that wants our life to be the best it can be. In that case, the search for Soul is a purposeful exchange of information between our unconscious mind, which knows what's best for us, and our conscious mind, which for some reason, continually gets lost in the complex, distracting influences of our everyday existence.

*The whole of life is symbolic because the whole of life has meaning.*

**Boris Pasternak, [Attr.]**

Whichever way you choose to think of the Soul influence, to find a meaningful purpose in life, you do have to accept, or at least assume, that there's more to life than you can see, touch, or feel. For many people, that's not a simple decision. If you're a physical, world-oriented, concrete thinker, uncomfortable with the concept of an unseen influence, let me assure you I have no intention of trying to convince you to believe differently. I do, however, have one suggestion.

I believe the greatest hindrance to happiness in today's world is narrowness of belief. Our world has become so complicated, and it changes so rapidly, it's nearly impossible to imagine any one person understanding it all. The only way to exist in the world is to adopt the best set of beliefs of "what is right" we can find and then continually reassess those beliefs as we discover new information. If the concept of Soul challenges you, face it as you would any other new concept. Be as skeptical as you wish, but never stop investigating. You'll find that simply being willing to consider will put you in touch with Soul as quickly as any other approach.

## Care of the Soul

If you're willing to consider the existence of Soul as possible, how should you approach its needs and demands? How do you care for something you can't touch, feel, or see? Like happiness, I can't describe for you exactly what your Soul will want from you. What I will try to describe is my own personal interpretation of what my Soul asks of me. To the greatest extent, I've apparently been able to satisfy my Soul's requests, and as a result, I've been able to find a great deal of happiness. If nothing else, I can give you an example how one successful person has taken the concept of Soul and integrated it into what was already a happy life.

I visualize Soul as a power, a force, almost a personality inside me that desires connection with everything that exists in the world around me. Sometimes I feel almost like an intermediary, a conduit for interaction between my Soul and the physical world. To use the symbol that I expect will be most familiar for you, I imagine Soul as my subconscious mind.

*Literature and butterflies are the two sweetest passions known to man.*

**Vladimir Nabokov, quoted in *Radio Times***

I honestly believe that deep inside each of us is the knowledge of what is right and what is wrong, not just on a large-scale, social-interaction basis, but on a private, personal level. You can call it your conscience if you want, but it's more than that. It's an innate sense of what will truly satisfy us and bring long-term happiness, as opposed to temporary entertainment. In other words, you really do already know what will bring you satisfaction in your life, and you actually know how to find it. The problem is that you don't know that you know.

Soul acts as an inner compass pointing you in the directions where important life issues lie. It's much more complicated than a compass, however, because it doesn't always point in the same direction. On some days, your job may hold important Soul benefits for your consideration. On other days, someone in your family may be carrying the key to Soul. Once in a while, Soul may simply be asking for a time of nothing, a period of sitting quietly and listening to the silence.

That, in its true essence, is the challenge of caring for the Soul and learning to read its compass as it swings from one life event to another. Care of the Soul is, more than anything else, recognition. Can you listen carefully enough to hear what it desires? Are you willing to accept its opinion that there's something you need to consider? Once you've recognized an issue, are you willing to allow yourself fully to feel the significance of the issue?

Take careful note of the last sentence. Caring for the Soul is recognition, acknowledgment, and acceptance of the "feel" of an issue. There is no implicit requirement to change in response to the issue, to agree that change is necessary, or even to react to the issue in any way whatsoever. Soul doesn't demand reaction, it only demands consideration. It requires you to live to the fullest by being at all times alive in the world. Soul will be interested in virtually everything that happens. It allows virtually nothing to be ignored.

*It isn't important to come out on top, what matters is to be the one who comes out alive.*

**Bertolt Brecht, *Jungle of the Cities***

So, you care for your Soul, and follow what is supposedly the best course for your own welfare, by being totally alive in the world. What does that mean? Good question. One starting point is to read *Care of the Soul* by Thomas Moore. If you're the "ready student," you'll find the book speaks to you in a clear voice.

But what if reading this book is as deep an investigation as interests you? While I think you're missing an opportunity, I'll give you one last brief bit of guidance myself. Then it's back to some final specific suggestions before I send you out into the world again.

## Alive in the World

Assume everything that happens is happening because you either want or need it to happen. (That allows both pleasant and unpleasant occurrences to have significance.) You're going to have to trust me; once you get the hang of it, you can find importance and meaning in everything if you pay attention. It's not easy, it takes concentration.

I've had two times in the last few years when, for weeks at a time, I was able to see meaning in absolutely everything. Those were exciting times. It was almost as if some power was sending me messages multiple times each day. Events leading up to this book occurred during one of those times. I had become very frustrated about the state of the world, and especially about the unhappiness and lack of direction I sensed in young people. I didn't know what I could do to contribute to a solution, and it hurt to feel so helpless.

It wasn't exactly a conscious request on my part, but I know I had reached the point where I was searching for a solution. In effect, I told my inner self, "I need help, tell me, what can I do?" Within a few days, the answers started coming. Within a week, Michele first suggested, "You should write a book."

My first success in "caring for Soul" was finding a way to ignore the fact that I wasn't exactly an expert. Who cares, I told myself, just write what you know. If it has value, someone will find it. I wrote the preface to the book the day after her suggestion. That's how you make things happen; just do it!

*Argue for your limitations, and sure enough, they're yours.*

**Richard Bach, *Illusions: Adventures of a Reluctant Messiah***

Once I started writing, it was like a library opened in my spare room. Every newspaper had an article relevant to what I was writing. Every meeting with my Junior Achievement students presented more issues. Books on my bookshelf almost fell into my hands by themselves. Hello, Thomas Moore! Everything I saw, heard, and thought about seemed to have importance to the effort I was making. It was a feeling of great personal significance. I was doing something with meaning. I was somebody who had a purpose.

You see the best effect of being in touch with Soul? Life takes on real meaning. That is what you're actually looking for, isn't it? If you were able to feel that things happening to you were not random, that by looking at life a little more closely you would find any number of surprising lessons, would you feel better about getting up in the morning?

And what about the bad times? Does living in acknowledgment of the concept of Soul make it any easier? I'm not sure. When I have bad days, I'm able to feel just as miserable as anyone else. At those times, it's really easy for me to question all this "theory" and decide it's garbage. Pain in the present is a lot more powerful than positive, motivational theory.

What does occur is more rapid and positive recovery after the immediate pain has diminished. Once the bad day/week/month has passed (and honestly, they do end), an understanding of Soul helps me to see the bad time for the learning experience it was. Trying to maintain a consciousness of Soul during the bad times means several things. It means at least acknowledging the possibility that the experience has some meaning and purpose, even while it's impossible to see it. Allowing Soul to exist as a part of the experience will allow you to see the meaning later when the pain is diminished.

Acknowledging Soul also means adopting a conscious effort not to pretend the problem doesn't exist. There is a lot of benefit in allowing yourself to feel bad. When times are tough, feeling guilty about feeling bad is ridiculous. I'm not suggesting that you wallow in despair, but I really believe Soul sometimes just wants to feel the experience of pain. There's a real possibility that allowing the feeling to be experienced will shorten the period that the pain has to exist.

## A Soul Summary

All of these ideas are important parts of "being alive in the world." If you're fully alive, you're going to feel everything more intensely, bad things as well as good. Yes, you're right. We're talking about a really frightening concept here. We're talking about risk. All the pages about being happy, all the background about Soul, all of it leads up to a really scary proposition. If you want to find happiness, if you want to be fully alive, if you want to acknowledge Soul and allow it more freedom to influence your life, you're going to have to open yourself up to your feelings more than you may want.

In a world that seems to attack from every direction, being fully alive means refusing to pretend that pain doesn't exist. It means accepting that life will present difficult challenges and that the only success in some circumstances may be survival and knowledge for the future. It means learning to control the tendency to blame or make excuses. Nothing is all someone else's fault or is fully beyond our control. Everything that happens occurs in one of the layers of our environment and therefore has some direct relationship on our individual lives.

*Bad things are not the worst things that can happen to us. NOTHING is the worst thing that can happen to us!*

**Richard Bach,**
***One***

So where's the positive aspect of being fully alive? If you accept the higher intensity of pain, what's the benefit? The greater the acknowledgment and acceptance of pain, the greater the capacity to experience beauty, joy, love, and yes, happiness. It's the obvious answer, isn't it? But no, it's not a simple answer. The path to greater happiness through deeper feeling, through becoming more fully alive, is not easy, it's not automatic, and it will not occur overnight. It is a path with a beginning, a length, and possibly no clear end.

*When you've parked the second car in the garage, and installed the hot tub, and skied in Colorado, and wind-surfed in the Caribbean, when you've had your first love affair and your second and your third, the question will remain, where does the dream end for me?*

**Mario Cuomo, Governor of NY, Commencement address at Syracuse University, quoted in *NY Times***

The actual benefit is that along the way, there are some beautiful views. There are things you will see that you wouldn't have noticed otherwise. If you're lucky, you may find enough things of beauty that you'll decide the trip was a good one, that the effort was quite worthwhile. If that occurs, you'll call it happiness. It won't be a destination, it won't be a place you reach where you can sit and relax in comfort. It will be a conclusion you reach looking back at where you've been.

The real goal is to be able to look back one day and say, "I'm pretty happy with the way my life has been going." It won't say anything about tomorrow, because Soul may still have some challenges waiting, but it will be a satisfaction that you've made real progress. No, happiness is not necessarily a state of being, it's more an assessment of past success in living life as it occurred. The satisfaction of knowing you did all right is, for me, the best measure of happiness and offers the promise that tomorrow has the potential to be all right, also. If that's not a perfectly wonderful, realistic, attainable definition of happiness, I don't know what else to offer.

*I'm never going to be a movie star. But then, in all probability, Liz Taylor is never going to teach first and second grade.*

**Mary J. Wilson, elementary school teacher,** ***Newsweek***

*Each handicap is like a hurdle in a steeplechase, and when you ride up to it, if you throw your heart over, the horse will go along, too.*

**Lawrence Bixby, "Comeback from a Brain Operation,"** ***Harper's***

*Failure is the condiment that gives success its flavor.*

**Truman Capote,** ***The Dogs Bark***

*As long as you are trying to be something other than what you actually are, your mind merely wears itself out. But if you say, 'this is what I am, it is a fact that I am going to investigate, understand,' then you can go beyond.*

**Krishnamurti, *The Penguin Krishnamurti Reader*, "Questions and Answers"**

# hapter 12

## Back to the Future

Welcome back to the real world. So what do you think about such a different way to approach life? Are you interested in trying to see things in a new way? If so, you're probably in for a bit of a challenge, but I believe it will be worthwhile. Now all we have to do is find a place for you to start.

I have the feeling it may not be appropriate to start with areas in your life that are causing you the most problems at the moment. Trying to apply new ways of dealing with life to complicated issues may be too much to ask at first. My plan, therefore, is to talk about aspects and activities in life that are good tests for using your "new eyes." We'll start with some of the easy tests and move along slowly.

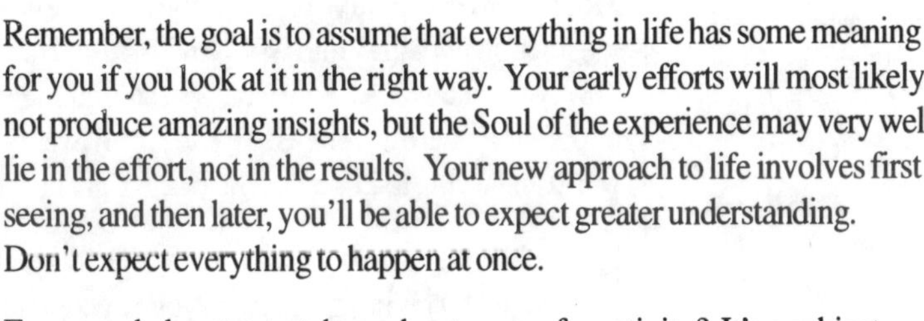

Remember, the goal is to assume that everything in life has some meaning for you if you look at it in the right way. Your early efforts will most likely not produce amazing insights, but the Soul of the experience may very well lie in the effort, not in the results. Your new approach to life involves first seeing, and then later, you'll be able to expect greater understanding. Don't expect everything to happen at once.

For a good place to start, how about areas of creativity? It's a subject that surely involves lots of "seeing," and there's seldom any problem in interpretation. What it means to you is the only "right or wrong" that will matter.

## Creativity

It will be difficult to find better opportunities for Soul experiences than you will find in this area. Creativity is probably the closest thing to positive Soul that I can imagine. When a person is engaged in an attempt to interpret or depict life in an artistic way, what's really happening is an effort to show the connections of one type of existence to another. More often than not, the artist is trying to recognize an emotion he or she is experiencing and then find a way to convert that emotion into a tangible, physical form.

This process is very close to my understanding of care of the Soul. Creativity is our effort to take one dimension of our existence, the invisible, indescribable feelings we experience, and convert it into the three dimensional, worldly existence that is more easily shared with others. If the Soul desires a closer connection to the "essence" of life, then the attempt to find that essence and distill it into forms more acceptable for consideration has to be an activity that has a lot of Soul in it.

One of the key words for an artist is sharing. Few artists create for the sole (Soul) purpose of enhancing their own understanding of life. Most are trying to act as interpreters for those of us in their audience. As a result, there is the opportunity to glimpse the Soul work of others. As you progress in this seeing process, you'll find that all Soul doesn't have to be totally self-generated.

The most immediate example of this sharing of Soul work is Thomas Moore's book. Based on my definition of creativity on the previous page, writing is clearly as creative an effort as any more "artistic" activity. Moore used his creative effort to convert a view of "how to achieve satisfaction with life" into words that are more easily shared with others. In very similar ways, that's what I'm attempting to do. I'm taking an impression of life developed (in part) from twenty-five years in the business world and trying to impart its flavor through the written word.

*A child becomes an adult when he realizes that he has a right not only to be right but to be wrong.*

**Thomas Szasz,**
***The Second Sin*,**
**"Childhood"**

I guess I could have tried other ways to accomplish the same thing. I could have begun by giving speeches to young people. I could have choreographed a dance set in a business environment. I could have composed a rock opera, created a comic strip, or become more involved in promoting "Take Your Daughter to Work Day." All would have been artistically creative and all would have been Soul experiences. Just as important, they all would have had the potential for providing opportunities for others to have Soul experiences.

That's the first easy lesson in your new effort to live more fully. A huge number of people in our world are putting tremendous emotional and physical energy into providing resources to help you care for your Soul. Your first step is no more complicated than taking a look at the first creative presentation that catches your eye and trying to imagine why it's there for you.

First, what was the artist trying to accomplish? If you had been standing next to the creator as the creation was coming to life, what would you have seen and felt? What essence of life was the artist trying to depict?

*The man who views the world at 50 the same as he did at 20 has wasted 30 years of his life.*

**Muhammed Ali, *Playboy***

Remember, there are no wrong answers! In fact, if you were truly able somehow to know exactly what the artist was trying to say, you would probably lose part of the benefit of the experience. It's most important to wonder a bit.

The greatest benefit will be if you end up unsure what the artist was feeling. You're then left to decide what the creation makes you feel. Such an experience makes you work backwards. In other words, you see the physical form of a Soul experience. What invisible, indescribable feeling in you could have inspired such a distilled result? Before you're done with the process, you will have afforded your Soul the opportunity to reexperience a number of Soul events through your memories. Through another's creativity, you've had the opportunity to consider a number of Soul issues. It may seem surprising, but I believe that secondhand Soul considerations may be just as valuable as firsthand experiences. And in some cases, they can be a lot safer!

## Taking Control of Your Life

For instance, living fully in today's world involves at least acknowledging the terrible violence and inequities in our society. Your Soul has every intention of dealing with those issues. Are you really interested in becoming a part of an environment where drugs and killing are a daily part of life? I hope not. But how can you face those issues without becoming a part of them? An approach through creativity can be the answer.

Even in the midst of the horror, there are artists attempting to do their own Soul work by communicating the pain they experience through their art. Your new eyes may be able to see beneath the surface of a painting, a dance, or a piece of music to experience secondhand the terror, the humiliation, or the hopelessness lived by the artist.

What will you gain through such an experience? If you assume that your Soul is going to lead you into ever-widening avenues of investigation, your artistic search may actually satisfy your Soul to the extent you never need to experience such a life firsthand. Yes, I guess it does seem laughable that this Soul of yours could ever lead you into unnecessary danger just for the experience, but I'm not sure I'd laugh too quickly.

How many times already in your young life have you done things more stupid than you can imagine? You knew better, it was clearly illogical to you even at the time, but it was "just something you couldn't seem to resist." The bad news is, it's not all the result of the impulsiveness of youth. You'll probably still do things like that as an adult. Call it what you will, but "your Soul's desire for experience" is as good an explanation as any other.

*Art does not reproduce what we see. It makes us see.*

**Paul Klee,**
***Creative Credo***

Your new consideration of life, and Soul, may actually be an opportunity to take back the control of your life. By negotiating with Soul for control of how you experience life, you decide what's necessary and what isn't. You decide where risk is appropriate and where it's not. Being fully alive in the world means that you can see further ahead along your path than you've been able to previously. It can be a wonderful feeling to make decisions for yourself about how you're going to live your life. Seeing more clearly, caring for your Soul, and, therefore, living more fully can help to give you that ability.

My more important desire on the subject of creativity is that you allow yourself access to the beauty of life that you can find through an artist's work. I've already stated that it's important to experience an artist's pain. I'll accept a need for Gangsta Rap, questionably pornographic art, and even the overwhelming tendency of modern music to concentrate on the "I love her, she left me, but somehow I'll get her back" ballads. If you need to experience pain, do as much of it secondhand as possible.

## Art/Music/Dance

Living life more fully, however, opens up for you access to the joys and beauties of life that you may sometimes wonder if you'll ever experience firsthand. If you've ever cried (or almost cried, anyway) at the beauty of a love story in a book, a movie, or a play, you understand the potential of secondhand happy experiences. Just think of the opportunities for greater happiness if you actually learned to feel happy through the artistic creations of others. No, it will never replace the real experiences you should strive to find, but you can enhance the quality of your life in a major way.

It's hard to decide what to recommend first. It may frustrate some of you, but I feel the best art for the purpose we're considering is the art that has lasted for centuries. Classical music, impressionist paintings, classical ballet, even the great works of literature have all inspired millions. I don't care how far they may seem from your experience or how little you think you'd like them, their appeal has lasted through social transitions just as traumatic as what we've experienced. They've retained the power to move people from every culture and background. A true appreciation for any of them can elevate the quality of a person's life.

I know it's ridiculous to suggest you can't find happiness unless you can appreciate "art." That's not at all what I'm trying to do. It is true, however, that my spirits can be uplifted to amazing heights simply by hearing a familiar piece of beautiful classical music on the radio in the car. I don't go to concerts, I don't study music in order to appreciate it better, I don't even play an instrument. But periodically, I am able to experience moments of great happiness when a vision of Soul that was transformed into physical existence years ago is presented to my Soul for its own current consideration. My Soul is always very grateful, and it showers me with good feelings in appreciation.

No, I really don't know what will work the same way for you. I am confident, however, that there is something out there that has the potential to be seen with your new eyes in a way that can bring satisfaction to your Soul. It may turn out to be one of the classical disciplines; you won't know unless you try. It may be Nature. Finding beauty on this earth and appreciating it to the fullest can fill your heart with happiness. It may be something I haven't imagined at all. There are just too many possibilities.

*The difference between a rut and a grave is the depth.*

**Gerald Burrill, retired Episcopal Bishop of Chicago, *Advance***

Bottom line, if you're willing to believe in the need to care for your Soul, if you're able to imagine the value of secondhand experience as a pathway to firsthand Soul satisfaction, you have an unlimited opportunity, right now in your present life, to find new roads to happiness. Once you accept that the gathering of material possessions will never be the only path to success, you'll realize that the ability to gather the Soul gifts created by others is one of the greatest opportunities you'll ever have in your search for happiness. Don't ignore the possibilities. Go for it!

# Exploring Your World

Being fully alive means going beyond the surface level of life. If you're like most people, your interaction with life can probably be compared to a flat stone thrown across the water. Periodically, you hit the surface, however, more often than not, you only skim across it, anxious to get on to the next contact. It's partly a function of the speed with which we live our lives. There's just so much to deal with, so many issues to face, so many

*It is not so important to be serious as it is to be serious about the important things. The monkey wears an expression of seriousness which would do credit to any college student, but the monkey is serious because he itches.*

**Robert M. Hutchins, Chancellor, University of Chicago, *Quote***

decisions to make. It seems almost an unjustifiable luxury to slow down long enough actually to think about any single issue.

The Soul is not satisfied by such high volume, low intensity experience. Whether you are facing good things or bad, Soul wants the opportunity for more thorough consideration, more time for reflection. Caring for your Soul will actually require you to slow down, at least in terms of how you think about things. Surprisingly, that's not as difficult as it sounds.

The best example I can use is the way most of us approach whatever effort we make to keep up with current events. We're so afraid of missing something, we look for media that can summarize everything in the most efficient manner. Whether it's the nightly TV news, the radio bulletins in the car, or the newspaper with no story longer than you can read in two minutes, it seems every news vehicle is closely attuned to our hectic world.

I have to admit, I try to read the paper every morning in 30 minutes at the breakfast table. True, by the time I get to work, I can discuss semi-intelligently whatever may be the hot topic of the day. However, were I to want to understand how any particular issue affected my life or to need to see how circumstances now became what they are, I'd be woefully short in information necessary to accomplish that. In other words, I do a good job of satisfying my intellectual desire to "be current," but I'm doing little to satisfy my Soul's desire to see the bigger picture, to take the wider view. I run the risk of my Soul deciding to take control and force me to deal with the issue more directly.

Actually, I have found a way to overcome part of this problem. Again, it's only an example, but the greatest media Soul resource I've found is the *Atlantic Monthly*. If you want to experience a magazine that approaches issues with Soul, the *Atlantic Monthly* will show you what I mean. It's actually one of the oldest magazines still in existence, having been founded in 1857. Somehow, it's been able to update itself as times have changed without losing its connection to its (and our) past.

When you read an article in the *Atlantic*, you'll seldom be able to finish it in less than ten minutes. Their major cover articles (one or two a month) usually take a good half hour to read. More important by far, though, the articles always seem to search for so much more than the "news" of the issue. I have to say that every article I've ever read in the magazine seemed to have been written by a true expert on the subject. What you can be sure of, in addition to important facts, is a powerful statement of the author's personal opinions about the issues involved.

*I long to accomplish a great and noble task, but it is my chief duty to accomplish small tasks as if they were great and noble.*

**Helen Keller, To a five-year-old, recalled on her death**

A measure of the Soul of the writing is the controversy often engendered by the articles. It's interesting to note that there can be multiple experts in every field, and they can certainly have widely varying opinions, even on what constitutes the "facts." Each month, the magazine prints letters written in response to previous months' articles. Most of the letters seem to come from other experts, or at least from people as knowledgeable about the field as the author. Many letters are themselves longer than the pieces you find in your daily newspaper. Usually, the original author gets a chance to reply to the letters that were printed. This point-counterpoint is the essence of Soul.

Reading the *Atlantic Monthly* will acquaint you with what I think the Soul desires in the consideration of current events. It's probably not sufficient as your only reading material, since it doesn't cover every issue every month, but it challenges you to learn how to look beneath the surface. It forces you to slow down, to think, to consider. It gives your Soul a chance to decide if you need to think about the issue even more. It's a "one piece of reading material on a desert isle" kind of magazine. You owe it to yourself to see what I mean.

I think I'll give you one specific example of an *Atlantic* article that provided me with more than simple information. As I mentioned at the beginning of this book, while I'm writing for you, those who I see as today's "best and brightest," I have a powerful concern for the young people your age who fall on the other end of the spectrum of opportunity. What I wish is that I could write something for those who will not be going to college, entering the business world, or maybe even finding an opportunity to move out of the environment where death by age twenty is an all too likely future.

The problem is I have no experience with those young people. I don't know what they face. I don't even know how to think about their lives. It's hurt me to feel so removed from their experience. I've felt that my Soul has wanted me to understand better. The *Atlantic* provided me with a beginning. Even today, I still remember their May 1994 cover story, "The Code of the Streets" by Elijah Anderson. It attempted to describe "how the inner-city environment fosters a need for respect and a self-image based on violence." It's a terribly sad and disturbing article, but it's the type of article that should be read by anyone desiring to live fully in this world.

The article gave me a framework for my first consideration of what it must be like to live in such an environment. No more, no less. It didn't tell me how to change it. It didn't even make me feel I have to change it myself.

But it did make it possible for the issue to work on itself in the back of my mind. The framework was what my Soul seemed to need. Someday, maybe I'll be able to understand and do something.

Am I happier because I read the article? No, it depressed me and frightened me. Will I be happier in the future because I read the article? I don't know, I can't predict. Maybe if I someday am able to do something to make a difference, I'll be happier. That's a possibility. Maybe understanding the alternative will make me better able to help you find the life you're striving to find. That would make me happy. Maybe, if nothing else, the article will help me focus more clearly on what is good, healthy, and positive in my own life as it exists right now. That will definitely make me happy.

That, my friends, is the nature of a Soul experience. It makes you feel something more deeply, and it opens up possibilities for your future. It's those multiple possibilities that bring multiple opportunities for happiness. It's not necessarily an easy trip, but it does produce results. Dig deeply when you face a Soul issue. The dividends will show up eventually.

*The affirmation of one's own life, happiness, growth, freedom is rooted in one's captivity to love, i.e., in care, respect, responsibility, and knowledge. If an individual is able to love productively, he loves himself too; if can love only others, he cannot love at all.*

**Erich Fromm,**
***The Art of Loving***

## Exploring Your Relationships

As you become more effective at being fully alive in the world, you'll find it easier and easier to see below the surface of the issues and events around you. The breakthrough will occur when it becomes a natural process to take note of something, to examine its surface level implications, to look for meaning beyond the obvious, and finally to ask why the event is occurring in your life at that time. No matter how good you get at the process, you won't always be able to answer the "why" question, but simply getting that far will give you an incredible increase in control of your life.

Another benefit will be an improvement in your ability to understand other people. Seeing below the surface will enable you to understand motivations more thoroughly. You'll be surprised how much easier it is to understand human nature than you thought. Developing the ability to understand why people do what they do gives you some interesting new options.

What I believe you'll find is another one of my great truths. "Everyone is doing the best they can, based on the way they believe the world works." If you can come to believe that, imagine the difference it will make in the way you view life. More important, imagine the way it will allow you to view the actions of others.

Remember what I said about the near impossibility of changing other people? If they're already doing the absolute best they can, based on their view of the world, what possible logic is there for them to change? Now you actually do have a concept for working to improve a relationship problem. If someone you care about or have to relate to doesn't see the world the way you do, you have two choices. First, maybe the way they view the world really is flawed. If so, it's a lot less threatening to try to convince them the world is different from what they believe. It's not that they are wrong, they're just looking at the world in the wrong way. That's not an impossible situation to change.

*It's all right letting yourself go, as long as you can get yourself back.*

**Mick Jagger, quoted in J. Green, *The Book of Rock Quotes***

The other alternative is that they're pretty much right about the way the world works. Then what? Change the world for them. No, I'm not kidding. Remember the discussion about environment. It's made up of layer after layer, each one existing in connection with the others. You and your "other" exist within a specific layer. That innermost layer shared between the two of you, even though affected by all other layers, is still pretty much under your control.

Start by remaking the way the world works within that layer. If necessary, make it an exceptional layer, with more beneficial, supportive rules than exist in the outer layers. Invest some Soul in the layer you both share. Maybe, one layer at a time, you actually can change the way the world works. At the very least, you and your other may develop a more mutually satisfying view of the world and find new common ground for deciding how your relationship can flourish.

# Exploring Yourself—Taking Responsibility

What's even more important than exploring your world and the people in it? While the process of caring for your Soul and living more fully in the world may help it happen almost automatically, you need to put some conscious effort into getting to know yourself. You'll never meet a more interesting person.

If I had to give you one suggestion about how to find happiness, that one would be quite simple. You need to know yourself in ways you've never before imagined. You need to come to appreciate yourself for the wonder you are. You need to realize the resources you have inside of you.

*It was revealed to me many years ago with conclusive certainty that I was a fool and that I had always been a fool. Since then I have been as happy as any man has a right to be.*

**Alistair Sim, *Time***

The concept "care of the Soul" offers you a new process by which you can get to know yourself better. My personal belief is that acknowledging the self-centered desires of your Soul may help you to accept the reality of your own primary motivations. Before you can begin to interact with the world on a "fully alive" basis, and especially before you can begin to analyze the motivations of others, you need to understand why you are who you are. The first step in that direction is to consider these words of Dr. M. Scott Peck, "Everything you do, you do for your own personal benefit and satisfaction."

The first implication of that statement is quite harsh. It can be read to say, "There are no selfless motivations." In other words, anything you do that you think is for someone else's benefit, is really done for your own benefit. I do think there's some logic to that concept.

If you do something for someone else because you really enjoy doing it, you can be considered to be acting to provide pleasure to yourself. If you provide assistance to someone for whom you've volunteered to accept responsibility (children, aged parents, ill relatives), you'll probably be willing to admit that you do it primarily because it makes you feel good about yourself. Even if, while resenting the action, you help someone because you're "obligated" to do it, it's probably not difficult to admit that you actually could stop providing the assistance quite easily. You only continue because making the change would cause you more pain than continuing, i.e., you continue because it minimizes your pain.

No, I don't think it's depressing to view our own motivations in such a self-centered way. In fact, accepting the idea that our first obligation is to ourselves and that no one else is going to accept responsibility for our happiness is the most important step in taking control of our own lives. If you can accept personal responsibility for your own welfare, you're off to a great start toward being happy.

*I am suspicious of guilt in myself and in other people: it is usually a way of not thinking, or of announcing one's own fine sensibilities the better to be rid of them fast.*

**Lillian Hellman, *Scoundrel Time***

The second important step is to learn to overcome guilt. It doesn't seem to be as large a problem in society as it once was (in fact, many people seem to have forgotten completely that the concept of guilt ever existed), but I still sense a lot of guilt in the mental attitude of your age group. Primarily, I'm concerned with your reactions to issues of grades, college and career choices, and lifestyle issues. At your age, without the benefit of years to find out things for yourself, you're understandably influenced greatly by the opinions of others. When you don't express agreement with others' opinions, or don't live up to their expectations, you often end up miserable and somehow feeling guilty for reasons that you don't really understand.

Often without realizing it, parents have the tendency to motivate through guilt. If you don't see things their way or do things they want you to do, it's easy for them to make you feel you're a "bad child." That may be a way to motivate a dog or a cat, but it's no way to train a person to make good decisions.

Society will often treat you the same way. Motivation by guilt is an easy, and sometimes effective, way to convince people what to do. However, making decisions based on guilt is the "minimizing pain" approach. You do what you're told because it is what you want to do, however, it's only the best choice because it makes you hurt less. That direction is certainly not on the path to happiness.

Your best approach to mature decision-making, and potential happiness, involves acknowledging that you are going to do what you want to do. Your decisions are your own. Even if you're told, "Do it my way, or get out of my house," deciding to stay is your decision. You're deciding to accept temporarily the protection of the household, and the rules that implies, until you're financially and emotionally able to decide something else is better for you.

Do you see how powerful it makes you to accept responsibility for your own decisions? You are in control, even if it doesn't appear that way to anyone else. That's a lesson that will be critically important to you for the rest of your life. No matter how bad things may get, no matter how hopeless things may seem, you will always have the right to make changes in your life. A decision not to make a change will be your decision, made for your own benefit.

Accepting responsibility for yourself is a heavy obligation, but it's the only way you'll ever be able to feel free and in control. I believe your Soul acts as if it understands that concept completely. Soul wants you to look carefully at life around you. It wants you to understand how every decision you make involves all the layers of your environment. Then it wants you, after deep and passionate consideration, to make a decision that is truly in your own best interest. It wants you to be the best, happiest, and most alive person you can be. It sounds to me that Soul just maybe does "have it all together." That sounds like a great approach to your search for happiness.

## Exploring Yourself— Why Am I Who I Am?

Do you need specific suggestions for getting to know yourself better? There are plenty of ways to get started. Another truth of life which I share with Thomas Moore and many others is that who you are (and what you believe about the way the world works) is a direct product of the beliefs of the people with whom you've spent your life, i.e., your family. Why not start to learn about yourself by talking with your family members about what they believe?

*It is much more difficult to judge oneself than to judge others.*

**Antoine De Saint-Exupéry, *The Little Prince***

The goal is not to reach some agreement on issues, but only to hear more clearly the background from which your own opinions have grown. Approach the exercise as a Listener. Hear your own history. If you find some things you hear distasteful, don't make a point of it. Your purpose is to learn more about you.

After hearing as much as you can, take some quiet time to think about what you heard. With what did you agree or disagree? Are you happy with those opinions? Why or why not? If you disagree with views of life that supposedly shaped your own, where did the differences start? Who else has influenced the development of your opinions? How much of what you believe really has come from your own experience?

*No one can solve problems for someone whose problem is that they don't want problems solved.*

**Richard Bach,** ***One***

Each day for the rest of your life, your opinions about right and wrong will develop and change. No matter how sure of yourself you are today, you'll think differently tomorrow, and probably feel just as confident that you've "now got it right." Viewing right and wrong as gradually shifting concepts, especially recognizing how your ideas will shift with experience, can open your eyes to the bigger picture of life.

Realizing that you are in great part a reflection of others suggests you continue to learn more about others. After looking carefully (and with understanding) at those around you, why not learn more about other peoples and cultures? How they live may be very different from the way you do, but what they believe about life may not be as different as you think. The more you know about the way other people think, the better able you'll be to consider your own opinions.

A good way to learn about other peoples is by studying their religions and their philosophies. You'll probably be surprised how interesting other cultures' belief systems really are. If you have friends from other cultures, talk to them about what they believe. If not, read passages from the sacred writings of other religions. It will do more to help you learn about yourself than you can imagine. Again, don't approach the effort as a desire to know which is "right." Feed your Soul with all the myriad experiences of the world's peoples. You may begin to feel the satisfaction of a full and contented Soul.

# Exploring Yourself—Looking Inside

Once you've developed a better understanding of those around you, both near and far, you're ready to get to know yourself. Looking at yourself objectively really can be quite difficult. It's a tough balancing act to be able to acknowledge your own limitations without losing sight of all the special talents, capabilities, and potentials you hold. It's every bit as inappropriate to underestimate your own value as it is to get carried away by an overblown ego.

One possible way to see inside yourself is through a guided exercise in self-discipline. Many people find yoga, meditation, karate, tai chi, or other similar training to be helpful in becoming more self-aware. The key to each is learning first to control the superficial demands of the body and the mind and then to channel those resources into the highest and best use. Each discipline would probably accept as one of its goals the desire to "become fully alive" in the world. Each will very likely put you in touch with aspects of Soul.

*One could do worse than be a swinger of birches.*

**Robert Frost, *Birches***

I believe the greatest benefit of any of these disciplines, or of any approach to getting to know yourself better, is the eventual realization of your true personal value and importance. One of the most serious hindrances to happiness in today's world is society's presentation of material possessions as the measurement of success. Learning to see beyond such self-defeating standards is virtually the only way you're ever going to give yourself an honest chance for happiness. Learning to appreciate yourself for who you are, not what you have, is the objective. Caring for your Soul will point you resolutely along the correct path.

## True Self-Appreciation

The real goal of the search for happiness is an honest appreciation of your own special value. Within your mind is the ability to learn more than you ever thought possible. Within your Soul is the desire to find meaning in every part of the world you inhabit. Within your heart is the respect for yourself and for others that only needs to be released.

Your effort to build a new life after college, or even now, if you're ready to start, will offer challenges that require different approaches than you've tried before. You'll find that the measurements of success you've been conditioned to expect are not the only ones that hold promise. I believe you'll find that happiness is not something you build around you like a shell, but a place you find inside yourself.

You'll also find that the search for that place of happiness is a lifelong endeavor. Some days that place will be easy to find, and some days you'll have reasons to doubt that it ever existed at all. But, like Camelot, once you've learned that it does exist, someplace, somewhere, you'll use that knowledge to make the daily search a happy pastime. It is the search that makes up the essence of life.

*Happiness isn't something you experience;*
*it's something you remember.*

**Oscar Levant, *Time***

*The greatest happiness you can have is knowing that you do*
*not necessarily require happiness.*

**William Saroyan, *News Summaries***

*Man's task in life is to give birth to himself.*

**Erich Fromm,** ***Man for Himself***

# Chapter 13

## Groundhog Day

Well, you've almost reached the end of the book, and the beginning of your new way of viewing life. What do you think? Did you realize that life was going to be such a challenge? And did you realize you had so many resources and such power to make it all you want it to be? Are you still looking forward to that time, with maybe a more realistic optimism than you had before you started? I hope so.

The way, then, that I'll leave you is with a story. It's a wonderfully funny story which serves as an example of many things. First, it's an example of "seeing more clearly," and "being more fully alive." Remember what I said about everything having meaning if you look closely enough. Finding deep significance in a funny movie is a good example. Second, finding answers when you need them is a benefit of being open to Soul. Finally, it's an example of something no less significant than a way to structure the rest of your life. Suggestions for that effort pop up in the strangest of places. All you have to do is watch for them.

*Groundhog Day* is a movie starring Bill Murray and Andie MacDowell. Murray plays Phil, a TV weatherman with a problem. MacDowell is Rita, a producer at the TV station where Phil works. Phil's problem is that once again, he's required to go to Punxsatawney, Pennsylvania to cover the Groundhog Day prediction by Punxsatawney Phil, the most famous weather predictor in Groundhog history. He's been doing it for years, and he hates the assignment with a passion. He feels it's a ridiculous assignment, beneath his dignity.

His bigger problem is his attitude about life. Phil is the quintessential smart-aleck. To him, all of life, and each person he meets, is little more than a joke. In a way, he's pretty harmless, but he's also occasionally disgusting, and he's clearly destined to play an insignificant role in life. All he seems to care about is degrading his assignment to cover Groundhog Day and making a move on Rita, whom he sees as a challenge.

After an embarrassing day in Punxsatawney with Rita and the cameraman, they're stranded by a surprise snowstorm. When Phil wakes up the next morning, to his astonishment, it's Groundhog Day all over again, and he's the only one who's aware of it. To his growing frustration, he finds it happens over and over, and he's forced by some hideous fate to do the Groundhog piece again and again. For him, it's truly a fate worse than death, and he finds that death is not even an option. No matter what he does to try to end it all, he wakes up the next morning and it's Groundhog Day again.

*We are all afraid - for our confidence, for the future, for the world. That is the nature of the human imagination. Yet every man, every civilization, has gone forward because of its engagement with what it has set itself to do.*

**J. Bronowski,**
***The Ascent of Man***

Once he's reconciled to his fate, he decides to make a game of it, pulling pranks, making fun of everyone, and trying to find some way to get Rita, who finds him totally disgusting, into his bed. For what must be hundreds of days, he schemes, plots, and maneuvers, finding out more and more about what Rita wants in a man.

Going back to the same piano teacher each day as a brand new student, he walks in each day playing better and better until he's almost a professional. Over time, he sees people hurt in accidents and adds prevention of those accidents to his daily schedule. Even though his conscious intentions are despicable, he gradually comes to care more and more about Rita. The hopelessness of his situation is that there's no way in a twenty-four hour time frame to trick Rita into thinking he's someone that he's not.

In a way that's hard for me to describe for you in words (find a copy of the movie), over the hundreds of depressing, frustrating days he faces, Phil begins to see that his only hope for bringing meaning to his existence is clear. After the daily pranks and deceptions lose their interest, after he finds what he needs most is for Rita to come to care for him honestly, the only peace he finds is in actually becoming the type of man she would want. It's only after he realizes that no matter how much he changes, one day is too little time to make her fall in love with him, that he finally stops working toward a result and just lives each day a little better than the previous one.

Because it's a movie, the ending is fairly predictable, but it's still a touching scene when the day finally comes that Phil has become the man Rita can love. Somehow, when she finally does stay the night with him, it seems (even to me, the audience) like the right thing for her to do. And when they wake up the next day, it is a new day, and for both of them, a new life.

I felt the significance of the movie immediately, but it took me about twenty-four hours to sort out most of the messages. For me, the primary message goes something like this:

Each day, when we wake up and put our feet on the floor, the day is basically little different from the previous one. We face all the same challenges. If nothing else, we face the challenge of dealing with the boredom of what can seem like meaningless, trivial tasks. Not surprisingly, it can become natural to hide the pain in dark humor and disrespect for others who seem happier and more successful than we are. Happiness can seem to exist only in the acquisition of attractive, physical pleasures, but these seem to run from us as quickly as we pursue them.

*Ah, but I was so much older then, / I'm so much younger than that now.*

**Bob Dylan, "My Back Pages"**

Such desperation drives many people to evil manipulation of others, or disdain for their very existence. But to a very few, another alternative finally begins to dawn. Maybe there are small things that can be accomplished each day that bring a tiny bit of meaning to the twenty-four hours. Maybe, while no one else will ever notice, I can change myself just a little bit. Maybe, over a long time, I can make myself into someone who will attract the beautiful things in life, instead of scaring them away.

Life is taking one day at a time, recognizing that getting through each nearly similar day is what life will basically be like, and accepting that happiness will grow a little bit at a time from making small improvements in ourselves and in our attitude. Only in such a way will life come to hold deeper meaning.

What I've tried to accomplish in this book is to help you see the way to make each of your days a little better than the one before. I've tried to help you see that there are no miraculous ways to find happiness overnight. But I've also tried to help you realize that happiness is not a goal reserved for those who have money, power, or even simply the prospects of a great job.

It doesn't matter who you are, or what you think your life will be like five years from now, it only matters that it's a little better tomorrow than it is today. That's so very easy to accomplish and is so clearly the basis for true happiness.

*Make voyages! - Attempt them! There's nothing else.*

**Tennessee Williams, *Camino Real***

I wish for you the best that your life can be. I can't promise it will be easy or that success on a material level is likely. I can't even promise that life will treat you fairly, however you choose to measure that concept. But I can promise that life does hold rewards for you. Some are there for the asking, some take a lot of work. Some will only have meaning and value if you choose to make them have meaning and value.

The rest of your life is there to make of it what you will. Make of it something very, very special.

*Do not despair - many are happy much of the time; more eat than starve, more are healthy than sick, more curable than dying; not so many dying as dead; and one of the thieves was saved. Hell's bells and all's well - half of the world is at peace with itself; and so is the other half; vast areas are unpolluted; millions of children grow up without suffering deprivation, and millions, while deprived, grow up without suffering cruelties, and millions, while deprived and cruelly treated, none the less grow up. No laughter is sad and many tears are joyful.*

**Tom Stoppard, *Jumpers***

# Appendix A

## Using a Personal Computer to Solve a Business Challenge

This is a story about how a little knowledge, a bit of ingenuity, and a simple personal computer solved a major business problem. It illustrates a number of the points I've made in the first section of this book.

1. Computers have become so powerful, they can do a lot of the jobs that used to require a mainframe computer.

2. Easily-available software is so well-designed and flexible that it can accomplish amazing things.

3. People with only a basic knowledge of computers can use them to solve major problems. All that's needed is a realization of the computer's capabilities, the ability to read and understand computer manuals, and a clear understanding of what needs to be accomplished.

I believe this story is a good example of how computers are used every day to address business challenges. Certainly, there are much more complicated examples, using much more complex computer resources, but I think you'll find this project reasonably easy to understand. It may even teach you some things that you can use in the future. Don't worry about understanding exactly how everything was done, concentrate more on what was accomplished. If you can get a feel for the circumstances of the business issue and an understanding of what was needed, you'll have gained the most important value of this example.

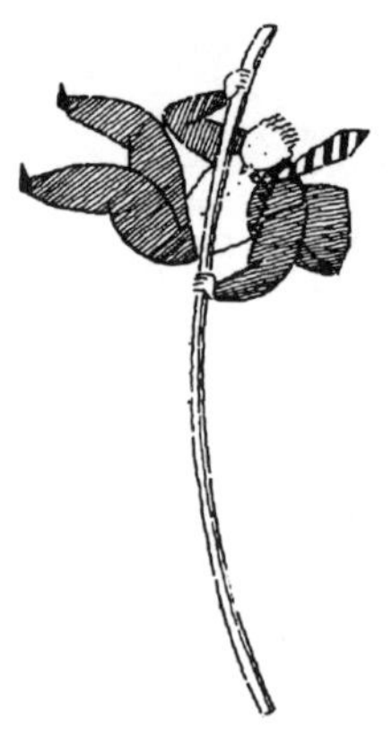

## The Challenge

One of the services my organization provides is management of several trust funds that provide health benefits for retirees of a major national industry. After the workers have qualified for a pension and have retired, if they (or their dependents) need to visit a doctor, go into the hospital, or have a prescription filled at the pharmacy, the majority of the costs of those services are paid for with money from the trust funds we manage. The money in those trust funds comes from the companies that operate in the industry that employed the workers when they were still active employees.

My organization was recently given the responsibility of managing a new health benefit plan that provides benefits for a very large number of retirees and dependents. My part of the assignment was to develop a way to bill and collect money from the companies responsible for funding the plan. The retirees in this new plan each had to be individually assigned to specific companies and the companies had to be billed for these individuals' benefits. Can you imagine carrying out such a job without the aid of computers?

*There are books in which the footnotes or comments scrawled by some reader's hand in the margin are more interesting than the text. The world is one of these books.*

**George Santayana, recalled on his death**

Fortunately for me, someone else was assigned the task of matching the beneficiaries with the specific companies. More than 80,000 individuals were assigned to almost 700 different companies who last employed the workers before they retired. I was told that there would be a computer tape of the 80,000+ individuals, along with the names and addresses of the specific companies to which they were assigned. The annual amount to bill for each assigned individual was also already established. "All" I had to do was take the list of 80,000 people and the list of 700 responsible companies and prepare bills. I would then need to be able on a regular basis to stay in contact with these companies advising them of changes in their obligations.

How many people do you think it should take to prepare complicated billings for 700 companies? How many people should be necessary to maintain data on the amounts these companies owe, to prepare communications about changes in these liabilities, and to send delinquency notices to companies which haven't made payments?

Would you believe, one, part time? Yes, while there are many people involved in managing the plan in one way or another, the part I've described was accomplished and has been maintained by one person, me, as a very small part of my duties.

# Managing Data by Computer

The activity I've described, maintaining a great deal of data about multiple similar entities, is exactly what a computer is designed to do. In this case, there were 700 companies, each with specific information such as name, identifying number, address, and responsible person. Related to each company was a quantity, representing the number of assigned retirees (and dependents). Each retiree had individual personal information such as name, social security number, date of birth, and dependents. The maintenance of this type of data is usually accomplished using what is called a "data base."

Large data bases are usually managed using a mainframe computer. The biggest problem in such an approach is the large effort to program such a system. It can take many months of effort to design a mainframe data base, and once it's implemented, it's hard to change. If certain capabilities weren't programmed into the system at the start, it's very difficult and time-consuming to make changes later. In the situation faced by my organization, we didn't have the time or the resources to design a new mainframe data base.

*Work is of two kinds: first, altering the position of matter at or near the earth's surface relative to other such matters: second, telling other people to do so.*

**Bertrand Russell, recalled on his death**

There are already many PC data base software programs on the market. Most of them are able to maintain the type of information I was going to be working with and may have been capable of supporting the needs I had. At that point, however, I didn't have the time, the knowledge, or the resources to research and purchase such software. I did, however, already have a good spreadsheet package (LOTUS) and a powerful word processing system (WordPerfect). I understood many of the capabilities of those software programs and felt sure I could find a way to use them to solve my problem.

## The Solution

My goal was to find a way to use the computer to calculate amounts due from each company and prepare the actual billing statements with a minimum of information needing to be manually entered on the PC. The solution would have to allow me to prepare regular communications to the companies advising them of any changes to their amounts due, again with minimal or no manual data entry. In addition to billing statements, letters to each company would need to include information specific to that individual company.

*If all the arts aspire to the condition of music, all the sciences aspire to the condition of mathematics.*
**George Santayana, *Observer*, "Sayings of the Week"**

The starting point was to get the computer tape into a usable format. Someone in our computer department converted the data on the tape into a format recognizable by LOTUS. Once the data was into the form of a LOTUS spreadsheet file, the information was laid out in separate rows and columns like a worksheet. Data for each company was on a single row, with separate information in each column. For instance, the first column had an identifying number for each company, the next column was the company name, and other columns each had information, like parts of the company address, the name of a company officer, or the number of retirees assigned to the company.

The power of a spreadsheet program such as LOTUS is that you can enter formulas in certain areas of the spreadsheet that use data from other portions of the spreadsheet in their calculations. I now had a spreadsheet with all the data on 700 companies that was needed to calculate the amount each company owed. The next necessary step was a way to make those calculations and put the results in the form of a bill to the company.

In a different area of the spreadsheet, I designed a billing statement. The basic form explained how the calculation of each company's liability was determined. In certain spots on that section of the spreadsheet, formulas were inserted to calculate the amount due based on certain data that varied for each company. At that point, the spreadsheet was set up to calculate the amount due from the company on the first row of the spreadsheet. As it was, it only calculated one bill and I had 700 to do.

The solution was to know that LOTUS had a special capability known as a Macro. That meant that it was possible to write a series of instructions to exist within the spreadsheet itself that told the spreadsheet how to perform a series of sequential steps. I knew it was possible, but I didn't know how to do that, either. That's what manuals are for.

Another several hours and I learned how to write a simple Macro. Now the spreadsheet had the ability to "find" the data for the first company, use it to calculate the amount due, and print the portion of the spreadsheet that now represented a company bill. Without stopping, the spreadsheet then went and "found" the data for the next company, made the appropriate calculations, replaced the first company's data in the billing section with the calculations for the second company, and printed the second bill. As I sat and watched, the computer spreadsheet took the data on the 700 companies and prepared and printed 700 bills. It was a really neat feeling to watch the computer "do its thing" as I lounged there in my chair enjoying a relaxing cup of coffee.

The next challenge was to prepare formal business letters to the companies explaining their obligations. The letters would need to have the company name and address at the top in a position to show through a window envelope so nobody would have to type addresses. The body of the letter needed to show the number of retirees assigned to the company and the dollar amount due. So how was I going to get the data in the LOTUS file into a letter format? Back to the manual.

*I've never been poor, only broke. Being poor is a frame of mind. Being broke is only a temporary situation.*

**Mike Todd,**
***Newsweek***

The word processing system I was most familiar with was WordPerfect. I knew there was a process known as a "merge," although I'd never tried it. Reading the manual, I discovered there was a way to have a WordPerfect file access a LOTUS file and pull data into the word processing document. Again, it took a few hours of study and experimentation, but before long, I found how to prepare one letter form (the merge document) and instruct it to access the LOTUS file I'd already been using (the source document).

With one set of commands, the merge then took place. The word processing file pulled information from the first line of the spreadsheet, placed the company name and address at the proper place in the letter form, put the name of the company officer at the proper place on the Dear (xxx): line, entered the number of retirees in the sentence needing that data, and actually calculated the amount due and placed it in the proper space. Then it "retrieved" the next company data, preparing a new letter form and entering the information as needed. As it completed each letter, it saved the resulting letter as part of a "target file." The result was a single word processing document that contained 700 letters to 700 companies with 700 different sets of information just waiting to be printed onto letterhead with a single command.

Want to know the actual computer time to carry out the two jobs? It took about two to three minutes each. Printing the bills and the letters took a few hours, but think of what it would have taken to type them individually. And don't forget, the printing effort only involved time and paper, no one had to "do" anything while the computer was printing the information. In addition, the results after all the letters and bills were printed for the companies were two files on the computer. No copies were needed for me to preserve a record of what was sent. Any time anyone needs a copy, I just print out whatever company's copy is needed. We don't have piles of paper lying around taking up space.

*Work . . . does not exist in a non-literate world . . . Where the whole man is involved there is no work.*

**Marshall McLuhan, *Understanding Media***

I still maintain the "source" LOTUS spreadsheet on the computer. Periodically, it gets updated with information such as which companies are making their payments or which companies have had changes in the number of retirees for whom they're responsible. At appropriate times, I can sort the spreadsheet to put all companies with certain matching characteristics together (non-payers, companies with changes, etc.) and send letters only to that subset of the companies. Working alone, I can prepare and mail letters to 100 companies, each with information specific to the individual company, in several hours. The computer part takes about five minutes; the rest is printing the letters, folding them, and putting them in envelopes.

## The Lesson

So what does this story teach you? As I discussed in the chapter on computers, you don't need to know how to build a computer, program it, or even to change how it operates in order to use it to meet very important business challenges. You need to understand a bit about how a computer operates, you need to have some basic familiarity with popular computer software like spreadsheet and word processing programs, and you need to have a problem that you understand thoroughly. Beyond that, you have to be comfortable enough to "play" with your computer until you can make it do what you want. I have to admit, it's not as much fun as training a dog to do tricks, but the computer will be much more dependable, and it won't chew up the furniture.

# Appendix B

## Junior Achievement and Its Programs

Junior Achievement is the world's largest and fastest growing non-profit economic education organization, reaching over 2.7 million elementary, middle and high school students in the United States and in more than 100 countries around the world annually. The 77-year-old organization's purpose is to educate and inspire young people to value free enterprise, understand business and economics and be workforce ready.

The programs span grades K-12 with age-appropriate curricula. They are designed to teach elementary students about their roles as individuals, workers and consumers and to prepare middle grade and high school students for key economic and workforce issues they will face. In addition to bringing the free enterprise system to life in the classroom, Junior Achievement programs teach youngsters the importance of staying in school. The organization also offers programs for youth who may have difficulty graduating from high school.

Through strategic business alliances in their cities, Junior Achievement's domestic affiliates (see list), have recruited more than 70,000 classroom volunteers to teach and interpret the economic education curriculum. These dedicated men and women who come from all walks of life include business people, retirees, and college students. The volunteers are truly the backbone of the organization, contributing more than 600,000 hours of their time to Junior Achievement each year.

For more information on how you can become involved in Junior Achievement either as a student or volunteer, you may consult the following list and contact the local Junior Achievement office in your area. Potential classroom volunteers are encouraged to call 1-800-THE-NEW JA. Also, please visit Junior Achievement's web site at http://www.ja.org.

# Junior Achievement Offices

| | | |
|---|---|---|
| **A** | Akron, OH | (330) 434-1875 |
| | Alaska | (907) 344-0101 |
| | Albany, NY | (518) 372-6465 |
| | Albuquerque, NM | (505) 262-0853 |
| | Allentown, PA | (610) 770-6223 |
| | Arkansas | (501) 280-9118 |
| | Ashland, KY | (606) 329-1699 |
| | Atlanta, GA | (404) 257-1932 |
| | Augusta, GA | (706) 722-8345 |
| | Austin, TX | (512) 837-5252 |
| **B** | Bakersfield, CA | (805) 328-9373 |
| | Baltimore, MD | (410) 527-1966 |
| | Baton Rouge, LA | (504) 769-6600 |
| | Battle Creek, MI | (616) 968-9188 |
| | Birmingham, AL | (205) 879-9365 |
| | Boise, ID | (208) 345-3990 |
| | Boston, MA | (617) 367-5850 |
| | Bowling Green, KY | (502) 782-0280 |
| | Brazoria County, TX | (409) 297-6411 |
| | Bridgeport, CT | (203) 382-0180 |
| | Buffalo, NY | (716) 853-1381 |
| **C** | Camden, NJ | (609) 222-1090 |
| | Canton, OH | (330) 455-5141 |
| | Cedar Rapids, IA | (319) 395-7903 |
| | Charleston, SC | (803) 745-1141 |
| | Charleston, WV | (304) 346-9753 |
| | Charlotte, NC | (704) 536-9668 |
| | Chattanooga, TN | (423) 892-4488 |
| | Chicago, IL | (312) 715-1300 |
| | Cincinnati, OH | (513) 821-7460 |
| | Cleveland, OH | (216) 861-8080 |
| | Cleveland, TN | (423) 476-6772 |
| | Cocoa Beach, FL | (407) 799-0222 |
| | Colorado Springs, CO | (719) 636-2474 |
| | Columbia, SC | (803) 252-1974 |
| | Columbus, OH | (614) 488-5373 |

| | | |
|---|---|---|
| **D** | Dallas, TX | (972) 690-8484 |
| | Davenport, IA | (319) 326-4080 |
| | Dayton, OH | (937) 228-7930 |
| | Decatur, AL | (205) 353-3573 |
| | Decatur, IL | (217) 428-2151 |
| | Denver, CO | (303) 534-5252 |
| | Des Moines, IA | (515) 279-9602 |
| | Detroit, MI | (313) 964-3000 |
| | Dubuque, IA | (319) 556-3933 |
| **E** | El Paso, TX | (915) 858-6771 |
| | Elizabeth, NJ | (908) 925-0046 |
| | Elkhart, IN | (219) 293-4554 |
| | Eugene, OR | (541) 687-8114 |
| | Evansville, IN | (812) 425-8152 |
| **F** | Fort Lauderdale, FL | (954) 782-3677 |
| | Fort Wayne, IN | (219) 484-2543 |
| | Fort Worth, TX | (817) 731-0838 |
| **G** | Grand Haven, MI | (616) 844-0800 |
| | Grand Rapids, MI | (616) 451-2674 |
| | Greensboro, NC | (910) 272-5134 |
| | Greenville, SC | (864) 235-9491 |
| **H** | Hamilton, OH | (513) 894-2055 |
| | Hartford, CT | (860) 525-4510 |
| | Honolulu, HI | (808) 524-2211 |
| | Houston, TX | (713) 682-4500 |
| | Huntsville, AL | (205) 533-4661 |
| **I** | Indianapolis, IN | (317) 634-3519 |
| **J** | JA International | (719) 540-0200 |
| | Jackson, MI | (517) 782-7822 |
| | Jacksonville, FL | (904) 727-7800 |
| **K** | Kalamazoo, MI | (616) 343-0860 |
| | Kansas City, MO | (816) 561-3558 |
| | Kingsport, TN | (423) 392-8841 |
| | Knoxville, TN | (423) 584-4359 |

| | | |
|---|---|---|
| **L** | Lafayette, IN | (765) 447-3549 |
| | Lancaster, PA | (717) 397-5779 |
| | Lanett, AL | (334) 644-4900 |
| | Lansing, MI | (517) 332-4585 |
| | Las Vegas, NV | (702) 362-8649 |
| | Lexington, KY | (606) 273-7737 |
| | Lima, OH | (419) 225-5816 |
| | Lincoln, NE | (402) 467-1010 |
| | Longview, TX | (903) 297-2202 |
| | Lorain, OH | (216) 329-3313 |
| | Los Angeles, CA | (213) 957-1818 |
| | Louisville, KY | (502) 425-8833 |
| | Lynchburg, VA | (804) 846-4813 |
| **M** | Manistee, MI | (616) 922-6317 |
| | Mansfield, OH | (419) 747-9337 |
| | Memphis, TN | (901) 366-7800 |
| | Miami, FL | (305) 534-1388 |
| | Middletown, OH | (513) 423-9776 |
| | Midland, MI | (517) 631-0162 |
| | Midland, TX | (915) 682-4966 |
| | Mississippi | (601) 948-3997 |
| | Mobile, AL | (334) 473-3901 |
| **N** | Naples, FL | (941) 649-6066 |
| | Nashville, TN | (615) 383-9500 |
| | New Bedford, MA | (508) 997-6536 |
| | New Haven, CT | (203) 265-5811 |
| | New Orleans, LA | (504) 832-0102 |
| | New York, NY | (212) 344-1033 |
| | Newark, NJ | (201) 645-5470 |
| | Norfolk, VA | (757) 455-9500 |
| **O** | Oklahoma City, OK | (405) 235-3399 |
| | Omaha, NE | (402) 333-6410 |
| | Orlando, FL | (407) 898-2121 |
| | Owensboro, KY | (502) 684-7291 |

| | | |
|---|---|---|
| **P** | Pensacola, FL | (904) 477-1420 |
| | Peoria, IL | (309) 673-0115 |
| | Philadelphia, PA | (610) 353-3090 |
| | Phoenix, AZ | (602) 271-4210 |
| | Pittsburgh, PA | (412) 281-7615 |
| | Portland, ME | (207) 885-5521 |
| | Portland, OR | (503) 238-6430 |
| | Princeton, NJ | (609) 987-0058 |
| | Providence, RI | (401) 331-3850 |
| **R** | Raleigh, NC | (919) 821-2100 |
| | Reading, PA | (610) 373-3500 |
| | Reno, NV | (702) 323-8084 |
| | Richmond, IN | (317) 962-0503 |
| | Richmond, VA | (804) 272-4545 |
| | Roanoke, VA | (540) 989-6392 |
| | Rochester, NY | (716) 327-7400 |
| | Rockford, IL | (815) 963-8413 |
| **S** | Sacramento, CA | (916) 648-1084 |
| | Saginaw, MI | (517) 752-9050 |
| | Salisbury, MD | (410) 742-8112 |
| | Salt Lake City, UT | (801) 355-5252 |
| | San Antonio, TX | (210) 490-2007 |
| | San Diego, CA | (619) 421-3020 |
| | San Francisco, CA | (415) 737-0370 |
| | San Jose, CA | (408) 988-8915 |
| | San Juan, PR | (787) 782-3044 |
| | Santa Rosa, CA | (707) 546-2578 |
| | Savannah, GA | (912) 651-0656 |
| | Scranton, PA | (717) 346-9080 |
| | Seattle, WA | (206) 296-2600 |
| | Shreveport, LA | (318) 861-1778 |
| | Sioux City, IA | (712) 255-3519 |
| | Sioux Falls, SD | (605) 336-7318 |
| | Spartanburg, SC | (864) 585-9381 |
| | Spokane, WA | (509) 624-7114 |
| | Springfield, IL | (217) 528-5252 |
| | Springfield, MA | (413) 525-5600 |

| | | |
|---|---|---|
| | Springfield, MO | (417) 886-2112 |
| | Springfield, OH | (937) 323-4725 |
| | St. Joseph/ Benton Harbor, MI | (616) 983-7579 |
| | St. Louis, MO | (314) 731-4000 |
| | St. Petersburg, FL | (813) 530-0884 |
| | Stamford, CT | (203) 327-2535 |
| | Stockton, CA | (209) 943-6610 |
| | Syracuse, NY | (315) 457-8917 |
| **T** | Tampa, FL | (813) 664-8930 |
| | Terre Haute, IN | (812) 232-6230 |
| | Toledo, OH | (419) 865-5511 |
| | Topeka, KS | (913) 235-3700 |
| | Tucson, AZ | (520) 792-2000 |
| | Tulsa, OK | (918) 664-8282 |
| | Twin Cities, MN | (612) 927-8354 |
| **W** | Warren/Youngstown, OH | (330) 539-5268 |
| | Washington, DC | (301) 229-5300 |
| | Waterloo, IA | (319) 266-1007 |
| | West Palm Beach, FL | (561) 840-8700 |
| | Westchester, NY | (914) 592-6040 |
| | Wichita, KS | (316) 267-2248 |
| | Wilmington, DE | (302) 654-4510 |
| | Winston-Salem, NC | (910) 727-2040 |
| | Wisconsin | (414) 352-5350 |
| | Worcester, MA | (508) 756-2207 |
| **Y** | York, PA | (717) 843-8028 |

# Recommended Reading


Adrienne, Carol and Redfield, James. *The Tenth Insight: An Experiential Guide*. New York: Warner Books, 1996.

Bouchard, Jerry. *Graduating to the 9-5 World*. Woodbridge, VA: Impact Publications, 1991.

Carter, Carol. *Graduating Into the 90's: Getting the Most Out of Your First Job After College*. New York: Farrar, Strauss & Giroux, 1993.

Chopra, Deepak. *The Way of the Wizard: Twenty Spiritual Lessons in Creating the Life You Want*. New York: Harmony Books, 1995.

Chopra, Deepak. *The Seven Spiritual Laws of Success: A Practical Guide to the Fulfillment of Your Dreams*. San Rafael, CA: Amber-Allen Publishing, 1993.

Csikszentmihalyi, Mihaly. *Creativity: Flow and the Psychology of Discovery and Invention*. New York: HarperCollins, 1996.

Csikszentmihalyi, Mihaly. *Flow: The Psychology of Optimal Experience*. New York: HarperCollins, 1990.

Fry, Ron. *Your First Job - For College Students and Anyone Preparing to Enter Today's Tough Job Market*. Hawthorne, NJ: Career Press, 1995.

Goleman, Daniel. *Emotional Intelligence: Why It Can Matter More Than IQ*. New York: Bantam Books, 1995.

Hillman, James. *The Soul's Code: In Search of Character and Calling*. New York: Random House, 1996.

Jensen, Eric. *Student Success Secrets*. Barron's Educational Series, 1996.

Moore, Thomas. *Care of the Soul: A Guide for Cultivating Depth and Sacredness in Everyday Life*. New York: HarperColins, 1992.

O'Brian, Patrick S. *Making College Count*. Green Bay, WI: Graphic Management Corp., 1996.

Peck, M. Scott. *The Road Less Traveled: A New Psychology of Love, Traditional Values and Spiritual Growth*. New York: Touchstone Books, 1988.

Pipher, Mary. *Reviving Ophelia: Saving the Selves of Adolescent Girls*. New York: Ballentine Books, 1994.

Pope, Loren. *Looking Beyond the Ivy League: Finding the College That's Right for You.* New York: Penguin USA, 1996

Redfield, James. *The Celestine Prophecy.* New York: Warner Books, 1993.

Redfield, James. *The Tenth Insight.* New York: Warner Books, 1996.

Robinson, Adam. *What Smart Students Know.* New York: Crown Trade Paperbacks, 1993.

Sinetar, Marsha. *Do What You Love: The Money Will Follow.* New York: Paulist Press, 1987.

Tannen, Deborah. *You Just Don't Understand: Women and Men in Conversation.* New York: Ballentine Books, 1990.

# About the Author

Alvin M. Stenzel is a writer (as well as a CPA and a corporate officer) in the Washington, D.C. area. His first book, *Approaching the CPA Examination: A Personal Guide to Examination Preparation* (John Wiley & Sons, New York), was an intimate, personal, motivational exploration of the mental, psychological, and physical preparations necessary to pass a major technical examination.

Mr. Stenzel has written articles for newspapers and trade journals, and has written and published a monthly newsletter on personal and spiritual issues. He has also written a number of short stories and has completed his first novel, *The Crystal Pond*.

Mr. Stenzel is a native of Portsmouth, Virginia. He is a Phi Beta Kappa graduate in mathematics from the University of Richmond (Richmond, Virginia). He has been active for many years in volunteer work, serving as CPR area coordinator and member of the Board of Directors for the American Heart Association in Richmond, VA, volunteer President of an employee credit union, founding board member of a professional educational society, and Treasurer of a United Way agency in Washington, D.C. He has also served twice as a Loaned Executive to the United Way campaign.

Mr. Stenzel is in his seventh year of working with Washington area high school students in the Junior Achievement program. In the High School Company Program, he guides students in the creation of their own corporation. Through hands-on experience, Mr. Stenzel helps students learn what to expect in the business world, aiding them in planning for college and building a successful future. Mr. Stenzel was Keynote Speaker at Junior Achievement of the National Capital Area's 1994 annual awards convocation and was nominated for the Maryland Governor's Volunteer Award.

# INDEX

## A



## B



## C



## D



## E

## S



## T



## U



## V



## W

# Notes

# DID YOU BORROW THIS BOOK?

You can have your own copy of ***The Best and Brightest High School Student's Guide***, so you can highlight the important parts and refer to it as needed. To order additional copies for yourself and your friends, please use this order form, or send all necessary information on a separate page. All orders processed using this form will result in a $2.00 donation to the Junior Achievement program closest to you. Thank you.

| Quantity | Title | Price | Total Price |
|---|---|---|---|
| ________ | **The Best and Brightest High School Student's Guide** | $12.95 | ________ |

**Sales Tax 5% of total above** ________

**Shipping & Handling $1.40 per book** ________

**Total Due ($15.00 per book)** ________

**Payment Details:**

[ ] **Check Enclosed with order.** [ ] **Please charge my credit card.**

[ ] **VISA** [ ] **MasterCard**

Number:________________________________ Exp. Date ____/____

Signature:________________________________

Ship to: ________________________________

Address: ________________________________

City: ____________________ State: __________ Zip: ____________

Make checks payable to: Best and Brightest
P.O. Box 34754
West Bethesda, MD 20827-4754

Also, look for *The Best and Brightest High School Student's Guide* at:
http://www.BESTANDBRIGHTEST.com
or
http://www.AMAZON.com
or call -800-247-6553

***Please inquire at the address above about quantity discounts and fundraising opportunities for your group.***

PREPWORKS
PUBLISHING